Parenting Young Children

Other works by the authors

The Parent's Handbook: Systematic Training for Effective Parenting (Don Dinkmeyer and Gary D. McKay)

The Parent's Guide: Systematic Training for Effective Parenting of Teens (Don Dinkmeyer and Gary D. McKay)

The Effective Parent (Don Dinkmeyer, Gary D. McKay, Don Dinkmeyer, Jr., James S. Dinkmeyer, and Joyce L. McKay)

PREP for Effective Family Living (Don Dinkmeyer, Gary D. McKay, Don Dinkmeyer, Jr., James S. Dinkmeyer, and Jon Carlson)

Time for a Better Marriage (Don Dinkmeyer and Jon Carlson)

The Encouragement Book (Don Dinkmeyer and Lewis E. Losoncy)

Raising a Responsible Child (Don Dinkmeyer and Gary D. McKay)

Taking Time for Love: How to Stay Happily Married (Don Dinkmeyer and Jon Carlson)

Parenting Young Children

Helpful strategies based on
Systematic Training for Effective Parenting (STEP)
for parents of children under six

Don Dinkmeyer, Ph.D.
Gary D. McKay, Ph.D.
James S. Dinkmeyer, M.A.

AGS®
American Guidance Service, Circle Pines, Minnesota 55014-1796

AGS staff participating in the development and production of this publication:

Project Team
Marjorie Lisovskis, Managing Editor
Mary Kaye Kuzma and Jill Rogness, Production Coordinators
Julie Nauman, Designer
Steven Moravetz, Marketing Associate

Product Development
Dorothy Chapman, Instructional Materials Director
Lynne Cromwell, Publishing Services Manager
Teri Mathews, Acquisitions Editor
Charles Pederson, Copy Editor
Maureen Wilson, Art Director

Project Editor
Mariellen Hanrahan

Cartoons
John Bush

Photographs
Mark Antman, The Image Works: p. 4. Elizabeth Crews, The Image Works: pp. 13, 71, 84. Don Dinkmeyer, Jr.: p. 7. Larry Douglas, amwest: p. 122. Svat Macha, amwest: p. 27. Jonathan A. Meyers, amwest: p. 66. Julie Nauman: p. 112. Steve Niedorf, Niedorf Photography: pp. 31, 34, 46, 50, 79, 104, 120, 131, 138. Alan Oddie, PhotoEdit: pp. 8, 128. David Shaffer, Shaffer Photography: p. 73. James L. Shaffer, Shaffer Photography: pp. 89, 97, 116. Michael Siluk: p. 56. Topham, The Image Works: p. 52. Jim West: p. 22.

This book is printed on recycled paper.

Printed in the United States of America.
A 0 9 8 7 6 5 4
Library of Congress Catalog Card Number: 89-85060
ISBN 0-88671-356-0

Contents

Acknowledgments

Parenting Young Children adapts and expands principles taught in *Systematic Training for Effective Parenting* (STEP)—*The Parent's Handbook* to the special challenges of living with babies, toddlers, and preschoolers. Many people contributed to the development and production of the book. We wish to acknowledge with appreciation:

E. Jane Dinkmeyer, Dr. Joyce L. McKay, Lyn Dinkmeyer, Dr. Don Dinkmeyer, Jr., and Deborah Dinkmeyer, who provided technical assistance and professional insight as well as love, support, and encouragement.

Our children, grandchildren, nieces, and nephews—Robert, Mike, Kristin, Jennifer, Luke, Joshua, Drew, Caitlin, and Stephanie Kay—the real "experts" on parent education.

The many early childhood and parent educators who provided valuable feedback in the early stages of development, including Lenore Green, Joanne Kresge, and Terri Wilson of Coral Springs, Florida; Connie Nink, Susan Severson, and Kay Stritzel of Tucson, Arizona; Dr. Marie Chittum, Fort Lauderdale, Florida; Lora McCoy, Pompano Beach, Florida; Carol Pehrson, Ludington, Michigan; Dr. Marion Rosen, Washington, D.C.; Judith Snyder, Cary, Illinois; and Dr. Frank Walton and Kathy Walton, Columbia, South Carolina. Special thanks to Kay Martin, director and teacher at Tucson's Adventure School, and Terry Webb, director of Saguaro Christian Church Infant Center in Tucson.

Mary Bregman, Coral Springs, Florida, who word-processed the manuscript through many drafts.

Norma Stevens, Tucson, Arizona, who provided secretarial assistance and offered insight into the early childhood years.

Flora Taylor, Minneapolis, Minnesota, who edited and prepared the book for field testing.

Elinor Bunch and Ruth Long of La Tijera Methodist Preschool in Los Angeles; Kathy Walton of Adlerian Child Care Centers, Inc. in Columbia, South Carolina; and the many other field testers who provided honest and helpful feedback regarding their experiences with the field-test edition of the book.

Dr. Douglas Powell, Professor in the Department of Child Development and Family Studies at Purdue University, West Lafayette, Indiana, who provided a thorough final critique of the book.

Freelance editor Mariellen Hanrahan of Minnetonka, Minnesota, who worked diligently to merge the work of many into a single clear voice.

John Bush, Minneapolis, Minnesota, who created the clever cartoon illustrations.

Finally, we thank the late Rudolf Dreikurs, from whom we learned much of what we know about parents and children.

Don Dinkmeyer, Sr.
Gary D. McKay
James S. Dinkmeyer
October, 1989

Introduction

Being a parent is both a joy and a challenge. No amount of planning or foresight can totally prepare you for the new world that awaits you with your first baby. When that baby arrives, your life is forever changed. You form a major love relationship with an unknown person—and make a lifetime commitment to someone you've just met! In your relationship with your child, you assume a new role that affects almost every part of your life.

During the first five years of life, children change rapidly and dramatically. Parents need to keep readjusting, too! When you finally get the baby to sleep through the night, she gives up her morning nap and upsets your routine. You wait for her to crawl, then find her the following week on top of the cupboard. She fusses while getting her teeth, but begins losing them when they've barely been used. Her favorite words change from "Mama" and "Dada" to "No!" Once she's able to, she asks hundreds of questions each day.

You are your child's first and most influential teacher. While learning to be flexible and adaptable to your everchanging child, you are also developing skills to guide and encourage your child as he grows. When he's a baby and you offer comfort when he cries, he begins to learn that he is valued and that people are trustworthy. When he's two years old and you remove him, kicking and screaming, from a store, he is learning limits. When he's five and you help him make a turn on his bike, he is learning problem-solving skills.

This is what *Parenting Young Children* is all about. Its purpose is to provide
- a look at the long-term goals of parenting
- information on how young children think, feel, and act
- skills that can increase your enjoyment and effectiveness as a parent
- skills that can develop your child's self-esteem and confidence
- support for yourself as a parent and as a person

The principles and skills in *Parenting Young Children* can help you feel more confident in your parenting role. The book suggests a consistent, positive, and democratic approach based on a program called STEP—*Systematic Training for Effective Parenting. Parenting Young Children* applies STEP's principles and methods to the special challenges of parenting infants, toddlers, and preschoolers. This book can be your partner as you work to build healthy patterns of belief and behavior in your young child—patterns that can form the foundation for a lifetime of positive growth.

Yes, parenting young children is a major challenge. But it is a challenge filled with opportunities for both parents and children to experience many joys and satisfactions. With *Parenting Young Children,* you can meet the challenge—and the opportunities—with confidence.

Don Dinkmeyer, Sr.
Gary D. McKay
James S. Dinkmeyer

CHAPTER 1

Understanding Young Children

For centuries, parents felt they'd accomplished a great deal if they managed to raise a child to adulthood. If their children survived disease, accidents, and violence, parents had succeeded at their job.

Today, children have the benefits of modern medicine and technology. But today's parents* have a more complicated vision. They wish to raise children who are

- responsible and cooperative
- courageous
- happy and capable of enjoying life
- successful
- respectful of others' feelings and property
- courteous and generous
- honest
- committed to love for home, family, and self
- able to get along with others
- self-reliant
- able to see opportunities in difficulties[1]

Quite a list! Yet, these goals will serve us well if we keep in mind that they are ideals meant to inspire and guide us—not to overwhelm us.

From the moment children are born, parents seek to shape and influence their behavior. But there are certain traits in each child that are part of a unique individual makeup—traits over which we as parents may have little or no control. As we work to instill cooperation, responsibility, and courage in our children, it will be helpful to understand these built-in factors and the role they play in shaping children's personalities.

The Basics—Special Traits in Each Child's Individual Makeup

Each child has a particular temperament, or way of behaving, and a particular rate and style of development. Raising a child means *working with* his or her individual qualities, not trying to change them.

---

*The word *parents* refers to mothers, fathers, guardians, or any other primary caregivers.

Temperament

According to some researchers, a baby is born with an individual temperament that stays basically the same throughout childhood.[2] Temperament has nothing to do with intelligence or talent. It has to do with unique qualities a child is born with.

Some children get hungry and sleepy at regular times; others are unpredictable. Some children easily accept loud noises, bright lights, and new tastes. Others may be upset by changes in their surroundings. Some children have long attention spans, some short. Each child's style or way of reacting is a reflection of temperament. We have to realize that, regarding some of their behavior, our children "just came that way."

By recognizing and accepting our child's temperament, we gain a deeper understanding of that child. This in turn can help us appreciate and work with our child's particular style.

Rate of Development

We help our children by respecting their rates of development.

Children develop at their own rates and in their own styles. They carry within them their own timetables for reaching developmental milestones. Cutting teeth is an event largely preset at birth. To a certain extent, starting to crawl, learning to talk, and being ready for toilet training are preset, too. But these tasks are also influenced by a child's environment. Developmental charts show the average age at which a child will do various tasks. (See Chart 1 at the end of this chapter.) The trouble is, *there are no average children*. Children can differ from the charts in some or all categories.

> At the mall, one-year-old Juan and his dad meet their neighbor Mrs. Robinson. "Is Juan talking yet?" asks Mrs. Robinson. "He can say a few words," Juan's dad answers. "But shouldn't he be doing more than that? Why, my little girl knew well over a dozen words at his age!" exclaims the neighbor. "Juan will talk more when he's ready," says Juan's dad.

We help our children by respecting their rates of development. It is our job to see, appreciate, and offer chances for development, not to push. This might mean we give our babies time and space on the floor so they can learn to crawl when they are ready. It doesn't mean we give them crawling lessons!

Style of Development

Children develop in their own styles. Some children learn with great enthusiasm. They practice in public, not bothered by their mistakes. Other children wait until they know a skill well before showing it. Some children happily babble nonsense syllables for months before saying a recognizable word. Some wait until they can put a sentence together before letting us hear their voices. Some children develop physically, emotionally, intellectually, and socially at the same time. Others develop skills in only one area at a time.

Stages of Development

Children develop in a predictable sequence. Certain kinds of learning must come before others. Sitting up and crawling will come before walking. Picking up cornflakes will come before printing letters. Playing *beside* other children will come before playing *with* them. Understanding the general sequence helps parents know what to get ready for and how to be helpful during that developmental challenge. But it is a *general* sequence. *Keep in mind that children develop at their own individual rates and in their own styles.* Each child will master a new skill when she or he is *ready*.

Babies Are Learning to Trust

Babies are learning to trust that another human being can be counted on for care, fun, protection, and limits. They are coming to know that someone will
- take care of their basic physical needs
- listen to their wails of protest
- stop them from moving toward danger

Babies are learning to trust themselves to take care of some of their own needs. They are recognizing that they can
- comfort themselves with a thumb or a special blanket
- get what they want by crawling and grasping
- enjoy *themselves,* finding their toes or fists to chew on

Babies are also learning to trust the world around them. They discover that the world is sometimes predictable and sometimes surprising, but basically safe.
- The floor is hard; stuffed animals aren't.
- Orange food tastes good; green food is "iffy."
- Water feels good; getting a shot hurts.

Toddlers Are Reaching for Independence

Once children have learned to trust, they can try independence. Knowing someone will be there for them, they feel freer to push away, experiment, make demands.

Toddlers search for independence in a variety of ways. Each act of independence teaches them about a human trait.

- They insist on doing everything for themselves (and are learning the trait of *self-reliance*).
- They claim all toys are "mine" (*ownership*).
- They become afraid of the dark or strangers (*insecurity*).
- They pet the cat gently (*self-control*).

In these and many other ways, toddlers are taking major steps in growing up.

Preschoolers Are Beginning to Show Creativity

Preschoolers have formed both trust and independence in their basic relationships. Now they are ready to plunge into a broader world of friends and toys. Preschoolers are artists, inventors, and manufacturers. Their inspirations, raw materials, and tools surround them in the form of books, dolls, building toys, balls, sand, water, paint, language, and playmates. They apply their vivid imaginations to all situations.

Preschoolers see themselves as adults when they play "house" or "school" or "doctor." They practice adult roles when they feed their dolls and make mud pies for lunch. They imitate adult adventure when they ride their trikes as fire engines and build forts from blankets. They also create pure fantasy worlds out of their surroundings. The bathtub becomes a monster's pool. A cardboard box becomes a castle. A playground becomes the surface of the moon.

Language is suddenly used for complicated stories. Preschoolers either make them up, or they beg you to read or tell them. Words themselves become fascinating. Children invent their own "silly" ones, rhyme for the fun of rhyming, and may feel the excitement of shocking adults with a swearword.

Preschoolers also need friends. They need to learn how people get along. With friends, they practice using ideas, making decisions, settling arguments, and showing appreciation.[3]

"Babies," "Toddlers," and "Preschoolers" Defined*

Parenting Young Children often refers to children as *babies (or infants), toddlers,* or *preschoolers.* Below are some very general definitions for children in each age group. These definitions are not intended to be rigid, but rather to provide a general framework for applying ideas about young children.

Babies (or Infants)—When we refer to *babies* or *infants,* we are including newborns, children who sit up, crawlers, creepers, and early walkers. In general, consider babyhood to end between the ages of fifteen and eighteen months.

Toddlers—The term *toddlers* refers to children who are quite mobile but not yet as adept with motor skills or language as preschoolers are. In general, consider a toddler to be between the ages of eighteen months and three years.

Preschoolers—*Preschoolers* are older than toddlers, but not yet school-aged. In general, consider a preschooler to be between the ages of three and five years.

*For more specific information about young children's development, see Chart 1, "A Look at Development from Birth Through Age Five."

Beyond the Basics—Your Role in Influencing Your Child's Behavior

Would life be different with a two-year-old if we had heard only about the "terrific twos"?

As you grow in recognizing and appreciating your child's unique temperament and developmental style, you can in turn grow in your effectiveness as a parent. There are many ways in which parents influence children. One way is by creating a home environment that is both accepting and encouraging. You might start by considering your own expectations.

The Power of Expectations

Most parents bring expectations to parenting. Often—perhaps too often—parents and professionals who work with young children focus on negative behavior. We hear and use terms such as "terrible twos," "rug rats," and "little monsters." No wonder we tend to expect the worst from children at certain ages!

Young children often sense our expectations and try to meet them. But consider this: Would life be different with a two-year-old if we had heard only about the "*terrific* twos"? Or if all we expected was cooperation and good behavior?

Labels can become self-fulfilling. Work to find positive expectations.

Expectations are powerful. The more positive your expectations are, the more likely you will get cooperation from your child.

More "Yes!"—Less "No!"

Most children start to use the magic word *no* when they are between eighteen and twenty-four months old. Some say no even when they really mean yes. *No* may be such a popular word with children because it's so popular with parents. The wise parent will look for ways to use the word *yes* more often.

> Two-year-old Paul is having a bad morning. First he grabs his sister's brand-new birthday gift. His mother exclaims, "No!" Next, seated in his high chair, he demands cookies for breakfast. His mother impatiently says, "No!" Finally, Paul demands to play with his toy train. Mother again says no, because it's time to leave the house.

Paul's mother says no three times in less than an hour. But she doesn't have to say it at all. When Paul grabs the birthday gift, she could instead take it away and give him something else to play with. When he screams for cookies, she could remove him from his chair until his food is ready and ignore any further outbursts. When Paul demands his toy train, she could say, "You can play with your train later."

Paul's mother might even go one step further and find a way to say yes to her son as she redirects his behavior. She might say, "Yes, I know you like your sister's present, but it belongs to her. Let's find something you can play with instead." Or, "Yes, I like cookies too! But what do we eat for breakfast?" She may continue to hear some grumbling from Paul. But Paul will be hearing friendly, positive responses. And, over time, his mother's focus on *yes* may well help bring on improved behavior.

Of course, there will be times when *no* is the necessary and wise thing to say. For example, if a toddler is reaching for the burners or knobs on the stove, his* parent might say, "No—never touch the stove." Then the parent can redirect the child to something else in the kitchen— perhaps give him some safe utensils to play with under the table. But work to use *yes,* rather than *no,* as often as possible.

*In *Parenting Young Children,* the use of masculine and feminine pronouns is varied throughout. The information presented, however, applies to children of either sex.

No may be such a popular word with children because it's so popular with parents.

Influencing Beliefs About Self and Behavior

All babies have the potential for building *positive* beliefs about themselves. Parents have great influence in this area.

When they have positive beliefs, children can be guided by parents to develop constructive behavior patterns. Then these patterns reinforce their positive beliefs. For example, parents teach that feelings are important by listening to their children's feelings and responding respectfully. "It hurts when Kitty scratches, doesn't it?" "You can hardly wait to get in the bathtub!" In turn, parents expect their own feelings to be respected. "I don't like biting—it hurts! Let's put you down and give you something else to bite."

It is natural for young children to be self-centered and unable to understand the feelings of others. Yet, from the beginning, parents can model and practice respect for feelings. Then, as children grow older and become more capable of seeing how others think and feel, an attitude of respect will be able to grow. As they experience positive regard for their feelings, children will grow in self-awareness and self-esteem. When they believe their feelings are worthy of respect, they will begin to learn to respect others' feelings, too. This takes place gradually, over many years. But the time to begin guiding children is when they are very young.

We are talking about a positive cycle of influence. Think of it as a circle in which positive beliefs cause positive behavior, which reinforces the beliefs, which strengthen the behavior. Through their own expectations and actions, parents play the major role in starting and maintaining this positive cycle.

The Power of Play

Beginning early in life, children move into the world of play. Playing is another important area in which parents can help children grow. To adults, play is something done as a change from their work. To children, play *is* their work.

Children must play in order to develop. In play, they learn about the world and their place in it. They practice the skills they will need as they grow. Through trial and error while playing, they learn about life.

Play with Your Child

Infants and toddlers, as well as preschoolers, can enjoy playing with parents in a variety of ways. Playing together helps establish a positive relationship, which is vital to help children learn.

Nora's mother spends some time each evening playing with her daughter. Eight-month-old Nora loves to play pat-a-cake and is learning to imitate the sounds and movements her mother makes.

———

After his nap, two-year-old Drew loves to play peek-a-boo with his dad. Dad hides his own face behind a blanket and then lowers it a bit at a time to peer at Drew. Drew reaches up to grab Dad's nose, but it's suddenly covered again with the blanket! Drew giggles in delight. Then Dad covers Drew's face momentarily, and the game begins again. Drew is learning a routine that's predictable and fun. He's also learning a few simple, unspoken rules about taking turns.

Some older children invent playmates. Such created playmates let children use their imaginations and practice social skills.

When four-year-old Gary drapes an old towel around his shoulders, he becomes a mighty superhero. To help him during his super adventures, Gary creates an imaginary friend named Max. Sometimes Gary shows Max his toys and introduces Max to all his stuffed animals.

Of course, children need opportunities to play without their parents. This gives them freedom to investigate and learn. Yet, it's important

for you to become involved when your child wants to involve you. At other times, too, playing with your child includes teaching a particular skill or helping her express emotions. Pretending to be an animal character or speaking through a puppet can help a child put feelings into words.

Choose Toys Carefully

Parents are bombarded with choices of toys for their children. The toys they select can help develop children's imagination and skills. Unfortunately, many toys do little to encourage positive growth—and some are even dangerous. Look for play materials for your child that are

- safe—fire-resistant, with no sharp edges or small parts that could be swallowed
- sturdy—so they won't break the first time they're used
- unstructured—at least some of the time, so children can be creative in using them (for example, blocks, sand, and art materials)
- age-appropriate—geared to the child's ability and development

---

Start Early to Set a Parenting Plan

It's often said that actions speak louder than words. As we think about what we want for our children and families, it can be helpful to have an overall plan for how we want to relate to our children. If we want children to grow up to be self-confident, responsible, and cooperative, we can consider what style of parenting will help them do this. A carefully chosen approach can guide us as we make decisions about day-to-day problems and challenges.

In the past, *autocratic* child rearing was the method most parents used, and this method is still common today. Autocratic parents depend on rewards and punishments to control children. A parent decides what is acceptable behavior and then rewards or punishes children accordingly. But rewards lead children to expect payment for "good" behavior. And when children are punished, they fear and resent the parent's reaction to "bad" behavior. Children need freedom in order to grow and learn. They also need the chance to make choices so they can learn limits and responsibility. The autocratic method offers neither freedom nor choices.

Permissive child rearing is another popular style of parenting. Because it is the opposite of the autocratic method, permissiveness would seem to be a sensible method. But it has its drawbacks. Permissive parents

A democratic family atmosphere allows young children freedom within limits. In this atmosphere, children learn that their choices count and carry responsibility.

set no limits on behavior. They offer children a great deal of freedom, but no responsibility. Society, however, sets up many limits and expects people to act responsibly. Children with no limits on their behavior will have difficulty learning how to behave in that society.

What approach to parenting *will* help us reach our goals? We think the *democratic* method is the most effective.

Democratic child rearing is based on equality and mutual respect. *Equality* means that parents and children are equal in human worth and dignity. Although we all have different abilities, responsibilities, and experiences, we are nonetheless all equally worthwhile as humans. The democratic method doesn't give young children the same privileges as older children or their parents. It *does* give their privileges equal consideration. It doesn't mean young children have a part in all decisions. It *does* mean that parents recognize the importance of their children's wishes. It means parents involve children in decision making when it is appropriate.

The democratic method aims to help children become responsible by setting limits for them and giving them choices within those limits.

> *Five-year-old Maria has the habit of leaving her toys and books all around the house. Her parents quietly explain to her that she is old enough to be responsible for picking up her things. They give her a choice: She can put her things away when she is through with each one, or she can pick them all up before supper. If she decides to wait until suppertime, everything will have to be picked up before she will be served the meal. If Maria forgets and comes to the table without having picked up, her parents will simply tell her she is not ready for supper. A few evenings of delaying her meal convinces Maria to get her things put away in advance.*

From babyhood through the start of elementary school, children have a strong need for boundaries and a limited ability to make choices. Very young children can't depend on themselves to keep the rules. They need someone else to set the boundaries and follow through with the consequences when they go beyond those boundaries. For example, a two-year-old left alone in a room with a plate of cookies can't be expected to ignore them till after dinner. He depends on someone else to put the cookies out of his reach.

A democratic family atmosphere allows young children freedom within limits. In this atmosphere, children learn that their choices count and carry responsibility.

In the coming chapters, you will explore many ways to guide your young child. The foundation for that guidance lies in your own understanding, example, and skills. It is from this base that you can sow the seeds of courage and cooperation.

Notes

1. T. Berry Brazelton, *To Listen to a Child: Understanding the Normal Problems of Growing Up* (Reading, Mass.: Addison-Wesley, 1984), p. 86.

2. Stella Chess and Alexander Thomas, *Know Your Child: An Authoritative Guide for Today's Parents* (New York: Basic Books, 1987), p. 13.

3. For additional discussion of young children's psychosocial development, see Erik H. Erickson, *Childhood and Society* (New York: Norton, 1964, 1986).

Activity for the Week

Examine your expectations for your child.
- Are your expectations positive? Negative? Realistic? Why do you think so?
- What changes would you like to make in your expectations?

You may want to write down your answers to help you discuss this activity at the next session.

Chart 1

A Look at Development from Birth Through Age Five

Note: This chart reflects the observations of several child development experts.* The "Qualities and Abilities" column lists positive qualities and describes what may be accomplished by the end of each period. However, every child is unique and may not match the chart. A child develops a skill when he or she is *ready*.

	What the Child Is Learning	Qualities and Abilities
Birth to 3 months	Trust, cooperation, and personal power (such as the effects of crying).	Gains head control, grasps and holds, makes sounds. Smiles fully, smiles in response to human contact. Shows distress, excitement, delight, boredom. Eats and sleeps in more organized way.
3 to 6 months	To affect the environment through body movements.	Sits supported. Has extended reach; grabs objects suddenly. Imitates sounds; orally shows likes and dislikes. Recognizes familiar objects. Is very social.
6 to 9 months	More awareness of consequences of own behavior.	Sits up, stands with assistance, crawls. Uses thumb and fingers to grasp small items. Drinks from cup. Has depth perception. Becomes more independent—resists pressure. Imitates behavior. May say "Mama" and "Dada." May recognize own name and word *no*. Notices others' feelings, particularly children—joins them if they cry or laugh. Is anxious about strangers; may be fearful of even the familiar.
9 to 12 months	More awareness of consequences of behavior.	May crawl up and down stairs. Stands. Is better at grasping and holding. Often cooperates in getting dressed. May say a few words. Shows and recognizes moods. Is aware of nonverbal communication. Is often affectionate. Is more assertive. Is afraid of strangers and of separation from mother.

*T. Berry Brazelton, *To Listen to a Child: Understanding the Normal Problems of Growing Up* (Reading, Mass.: Addison-Wesley, 1984), pp. 157-65; Theresa Caplan and Frank Caplan, *The Early Childhood Years* (New York: Perigee Books, 1983), pp. 20-21, 122-23, 148-49, 172-73, 198-99, 232-33, 266-67; Fitzhugh Dodson and Ann Alexander, *Your Child: Birth to Age Six* (New York: Fireside, 1986), pp. 51-63, 179; Adrienne Popper, *Parents: Book for the Toddler Years* (New York: Ballantine Books, 1986), pp. 277-78; Benjamin Spock and Michael B. Rothenberg, *Dr. Spock's Baby and Child Care*, 40th anniversary ed. (New York: Dutton, 1985), pp. 261-62, 286-87, 292-93, 307-9, 370-71, 376-77; Burton L. White, *The First Three Years of Life* (New York: Avon Books, 1975), pp. 158, 258-59.

Chart 1

	What the Child Is Learning	Qualities and Abilities
Ones	Beginnings of self-confidence.	Walks (usually by 15th month). Explores; empties and fills things; drops and throws things. Feeds self. Wants to be both independent and dependent. Uses clearer language. Becomes a toddler.
Twos	More self-confidence and mastery.	Becomes more independent—wants to do things own way. At times, wants to return to babyhood. Navigates without bumping into things. Speaks in 2- to 4-word sentences. Starts asking "what" and "why" questions. Has longer attention span and memory. Likes to help. Starts to play alongside other children. Gets greater bowel and bladder control.
Threes	More sociability.	Becomes more cooperative. Coordination greatly improves in gross and fine motor skills. Is talkative; enjoys hearing stories. Wants to be like parents. Recognizes sex differences. Picks clothes and dresses self. Likes being with peers. Learns to take turns and share. Begins to understand ideas of yesterday, today, and tomorrow.
Fours	To refine previously learned abilities.	Prefers children over adults. May have imaginary friends. Prefers same-sex playmates. Has firm sense of home and family. Is very active—runs, jumps, climbs. Fine motor abilities increase. Likes to talk, express ideas, and ask complicated questions. Most have good bladder and bowel control, but may have accidents. Awareness of time grows.
Fives	To adapt to the world of childhood and formalized education.	Begins to care about other children's opinions. Has more advanced reasoning powers. Has good control of hands and legs; eye-hand coordination is not fully developed—has accidents involving hands. Establishes handedness. Is talkative, with good vocabulary. Is affectionate and helpful to parents. Likes to make friends. Plays with both sexes. Develops sense of fairness. Wants to be independent and to be treated as if grown up.

Points to Remember

1. Parents want many things for their children—particularly that they be courageous, cooperative, and responsible.

2. Each child is born with an individual temperament. Accept a child's temperament and build on it.

3. Each child goes through stages of development at an individual rate and in a particular style.

4. Children master new skills when they are ready.
   - Babies learn to trust other humans, themselves, and the world around them.
   - Toddlers try independence.
   - Preschoolers create their own worlds, practice adult roles, play with language, and learn to get along with other children.

5. Parents tend to bring expectations to their parenting. Children sense that and often react as expected.

6. Find and create opportunities to say *yes* rather than *no*.

7. Encourage children's *positive* beliefs about themselves by helping them respect themselves and others. Positive beliefs will lead to positive behavior patterns.

8. Give children time to play. Play is their work, and they must do it to develop and grow.

9. A democratic family atmosphere teaches children respect for self and others and builds responsibility by providing freedom within limits.

Relieving Your Stress

Being a parent is a twenty-four-hour-a-day, seven-day-a-week job. It's no wonder, then, if we find ourselves under stress some of the time! Stress is a physical and emotional response to events we find upsetting. There are several ways to ease and handle stress that you may wish to use in the coming weeks:

1. Use deep breathing for about fifteen seconds. Let your breathing pace itself—don't force it. Practice silently saying "calm" as you breathe in and "down" as you breathe out until you begin to feel relaxed.

2. Use positive self-talk. Say simple, upbeat statements: "Be calm." "Take it easy." "You're okay."

3. Prepare yourself for a situation you think might be stressful. Take a few deep breaths and talk to yourself *before* facing the situation.

4. Think of a situation as an opportunity or a challenge, rather than as something stressful or something you can't handle.

5. Every day, accept yourself and take time to concentrate on your positive qualities. Make self-affirming statements: "I'm capable." "I'm worthwhile." "I make my own decisions."

Take a few moments now to jot down some affirming statements about *your* positive beliefs and behaviors.

Begin practicing stress reduction this week.

To learn more about handling stress, read Edward Charlesworth and Ronald Nathan, *Stress Management* (New York: Atheneum, 1985).

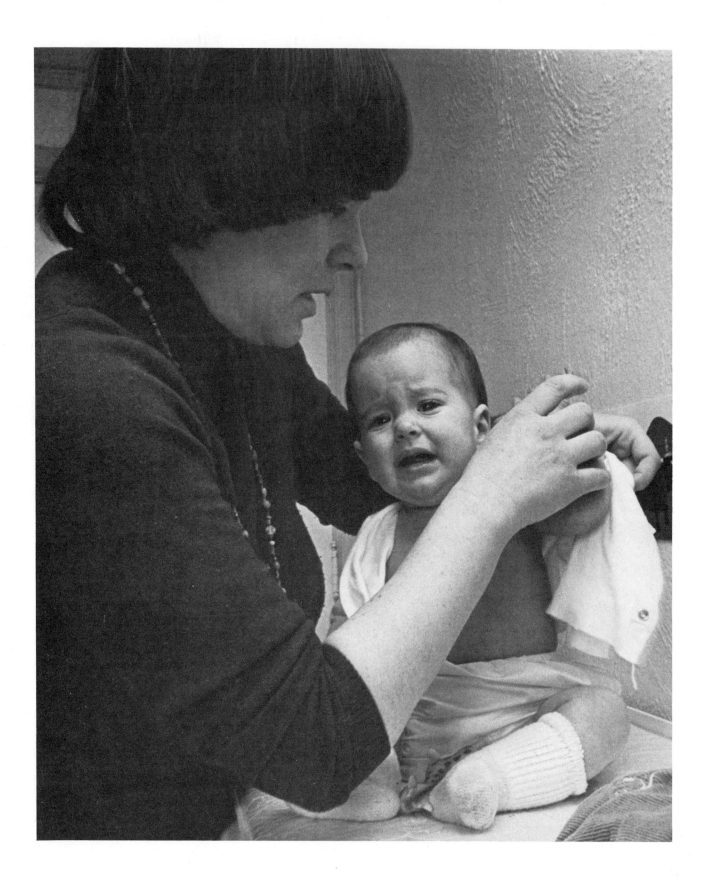

CHAPTER 2

Understanding Young Children's Behavior

The dentist is visiting four-year-old Tessa's preschool. Tessa and her friend Donnie sit side by side watching the dentist scrub a giant-sized set of teeth with a big toothbrush. "Who will come sit on this stool and let me floss their teeth so everyone can see?" the dentist asks. "I will! I will!" shouts Donnie, and he rushes happily forward. Donnie can hardly sit still or keep from smiling as the dentist flosses his teeth and explains to the other children what she is doing. Tessa looks on quietly, with great interest. As she watches, she holds her own hands up to her mouth and imitates the dentist's movements.

Tessa and Donnie have two different personalities. Donnie appears outgoing, enthusiastic, ready to step into new situations and take the limelight. Tessa joins in a different way: by observing intently and practicing what she sees. By their behavior in this situation, Donnie and Tessa are demonstrating their own attitudes, or *beliefs,* about the world and their place in it.

How Children Develop a Lifestyle

Starting in infancy, we all develop beliefs about who we are, who other people are, what is important in life, and how to belong. According to Alfred Adler, a pioneer in personality theory, the beliefs we develop and our ways of living out these beliefs form the basis of our *lifestyle.*[1] Lifestyle is the characteristic pattern of our beliefs, which influences our behavior.

Lifestyle is usually formed between the ages of four and six. By then, a child has developed a personal point of view about life and his place in it. Like Tessa, he may find the world fascinating and feel comfortable learning by observing and quietly experimenting. Or, like Donnie, he may rush into new situations with enthusiasm, expecting to be accepted and to enjoy himself. Both Tessa and Donnie appear to believe the world is basically friendly and that they find their place by cooperation. Other children may form different views. Some may believe the world is unfriendly and seek a place through force, through avoiding others, or by being afraid.

Everyone's lifestyle contains some faulty beliefs. Children often come to wrong conclusions because their experience is limited. For example, if a young child is always warned, "No, you're too little!" "You'll get hurt!" "Please be careful!" the child may decide, "The world is a scary place, and I can't trust myself." This conclusion fits with the child's limited experience, but as a generalization, it is exaggerated.

Because of our beliefs, we expect certain things to happen. And we often get what we expect. For example, the child who thinks people are basically friendly will tend to approach people in a friendly way, and will often get friendly responses in return. Our beliefs may influence others' reactions toward us. Then those reactions in turn may reinforce our beliefs.

Children, and adults as well, are frequently unaware of their specific lifestyle beliefs. Yet we all act on those beliefs.

Five major factors influence the development of lifestyle: heredity, the family atmosphere and values, the child's role models, methods of parenting, and the child's position in the family. Let's look at each of these.

Starting in infancy, we all develop beliefs about who we are, who other people are, what is important in life, and how to belong.

Heredity

A child's inherited physical traits influence lifestyle. Size, coordination, and physical appearance can be advantages or disadvantages. But either way, those traits do influence a child's beliefs about self. While every child inherits a certain potential, it is the child's beliefs that will determine when and how she *acts* on that potential.

Family Atmosphere and Values

The family atmosphere is the general relationship climate in the home. It is set by the parents. An atmosphere can range from warm to cold, cooperative to competitive, loving to rejecting, strict to relaxed, orderly to disorganized, discouraging to encouraging. The family atmosphere is a model of human relationships for children.

The family atmosphere is largely set by family *values*. A family value is anything that is important to the parents. They don't have to agree on the issue, but it does have to be important to each in some way.

> *Lois and Ted are both athletic and are raising their children, two-year-old Stephanie and three-year-old Sara, to be physically active. For Lois, much of the enjoyment of sports lies in competition. Whether running in a marathon or*

playing softball, Lois likes to win. Ted enjoys exercise for its own sake. He's more likely to jog or ride a bike on his own than to compete. Because athletics are important to Ted and Lois, sports has become a family value that will be important to their daughters as well. As they grow older, the children may choose to be active in competitive or noncompetitive sports, or they may do some of each. One or both of the girls might even reject physical activity, and pursue less active pastimes. Whatever activities Sara and Stephanie choose, sports will be a value in their lives. They will make decisions about how and if they participate in sports.

Role Models

Children model themselves after the important adults in their lives. They pay great attention to the behavior of grown-ups, and they imitate it. We may preach certain values, but if our actions don't match our words, our behavior is what our children will "listen to."

Young children learn from their parents and other adults what it means to be a woman or a man. They also learn about relationships between men and women. When parents respect and value each other, their children learn about equality.

Methods of Parenting

Chapter 1 discussed autocratic, permissive, and democratic parenting methods and possible effects each method might have on children. One of the things affected will be the lifestyle beliefs children form. How parents train their children gives children a model of adult-child relationships. If children are reared in an atmosphere of respect and cooperation, they are likely to adopt respect and cooperation as values and use them in other relationships.

Position in the Family

Where a child comes in the birth order of the family—only child, oldest, second, middle, or youngest—also influences the child's beliefs about himself. Sometimes, because of the number of years between them, children will assume a psychological position different from their actual birth-order position.

Elena (age ten), Tomás (age four), and Alfonso (age two) are siblings. Elena is the oldest child in birth order, but because of the number of years separating her and Tomás, she is, for all practical purposes, an only child. Tomás is the middle

If children are reared in an atmosphere of respect and cooperation, they are likely to adopt respect and cooperation as values and use them in other relationships.

child in birth order, but he may feel psychologically the older child of two in relation to Alfonso.

Actual and psychological positions can also change with the addition of new siblings through a parent's remarriage or through adoption.

Each child's psychological position depends both on the actual birth-order position and on the child's point of view as she makes a place for herself in the family. For example, in a family that values sports achievement, a second child may become a leader on the playing field and then carry through this leadership role at home—becoming the oldest psychologically. The way her sisters and brothers behave as they search for their places will influence this, too. All these factors influence a child's lifestyle beliefs.

More About Birth Order

Children's psychological position is important because children are likely to transfer their beliefs about themselves, influenced by their place in the family, to their place in the greater world. There are strengths and advantages to each position:
- Only children may become particularly resourceful because they spend more time alone.
- Oldest children may develop a strong sense of responsibility.
- Second children often learn to be cooperative and sociable.
- Middle children may be concerned with fairness.
- Youngest children can benefit from the sense of security that comes from having other family members for emotional and physical support. They learn how to relate with and influence others.

But there are birth-order "traps" as well. Children sometimes develop a pattern of using their birth-order position in negative ways. For example, the youngest child may want to be the "baby" for as long as possible, avoiding the responsibilities that go along with being a part of a family or other group. Kathy Walton of the Adlerian Child Care Centers in Columbia, South Carolina, offers some practical tips to help parents avoid the "traps" of birth order:
- Avoid referring to the youngest child as the baby.
- Give the youngest child responsibilities—ask her to do chores and be a helper.
- Avoid always referring to the oldest child first.
- Realize that a child care situation can help oldest and only children learn give-and-take with other children.
- Be aware that middle children are often sensitive—you needn't be impressed by their bids for pity or sympathy.
- Plan time to do things with each child individually to reduce competition for your attention.

These five factors—heredity, family atmosphere and values, role models, methods of parenting, and position in the family—influence who our children think they are, how they think people get along, and what they think is worth working for. As parents, we largely set family atmosphere and values, role models, and methods of parenting. Heredity and family position are set by other forces. But we influence these factors when we accept our children as they are and work respectfully with their strengths and limitations.

Why Children Behave as They Do

At the same time children are developing lifestyle beliefs, they are developing patterns of behavior. Most behavior has a social purpose. We all want to find a social place, *to belong*. Children need to belong. Early childhood is a time of discovering *how* to belong. As young children grow and develop, they discover that certain responses from others give them a feeling of belonging. They also learn that they can get those responses by both cooperative and uncooperative behavior.

Jason, age two-and-a-half, wants to belong by helping his dad wash the car. Jason takes the sponge from the bucket of water and slaps it on the side of the car. With a big smile, he says, "I wash the car with Daddy." Recognizing Jason's need to feel included, his dad says, "I like your help. You're getting the car good and clean." Jason feels valuable to his dad and starts to see himself as a helpful person.

This experience will influence Jason as he builds positive patterns of behavior that will help him find and keep his social place.

Rudolf Dreikurs extended the work of Adler, especially in the field of parenting. According to him, children will try to belong in positive ways. If they are unsuccessful in those attempts, they will seek to belong through misbehavior. Children misbehave when they become discouraged and think they can't belong by being cooperative.[2]

With this in mind, let's look at Jason again. At another time, Jason's dad might not recognize what Jason wants in this situation, or he might not have time to give him what he wants. He might respond, "You're too little to help. I want to do this by myself. Go and play in the backyard." Jason might choose to protest loudly. He might grab the hose and squirt his dad and the car. He might go to the backyard and find some way to be destructive that will bring his dad running to him. With any of these choices, Jason will still be pursuing his social purpose—trying to belong. His dad will be forced to deal with him and try to correct his negative behavior. And Jason will have shown that he is capable of getting his dad involved with him. That, too, is a way to belong. The next time Jason wants to feel included, he may remember the satisfaction of winning a place through negative behavior.

Dreikurs observed that children's misbehavior falls into four broad categories. Because the categories represent things the child wants to happen, he called them *goals*. The four goals of misbehavior are *attention, power, revenge,* and *display of inadequacy.* Each of these goals has to do with pursuing social purpose (finding a way to belong).

What Is "Misbehavior"?

When Dreikurs spoke of misbehavior, he was talking about behavior that comes from failing to find a social place through cooperative methods. But not everything we commonly call "misbehavior" is tied to this definition. To determine whether a child's actions can be considered "misbehavior," parents must first consider developmental factors. For example, when a nine-month-old child pulls a cat's tail, he is not demanding power. He is simply demonstrating normal curiosity. When a fourteen-month-old dives for the dirt in a potted plant, it may be the feel of the dirt she wants, rather than attention. When a two-year-old becomes unruly at a party, the reason may be overstimulation, rather than any of the four goals of misbehavior.

At times, children "misbehave" because they are curious, tired, sick, hungry, bored, clumsy, trying to be helpful, ignorant of the rules, and on and on. The behavior we find troublesome may not really be misbehavior: we may simply have unrealistic expectations. (Chart 1 in the first chapter points out general qualities and abilities of children at different ages.)

> *Three-year-old Hector ties a rope around his cat's neck and drags it for a walk behind his trike. Hector just wants to share his fun with his pet.*
>
> ——
>
> *Five-year-old Naima crosses the busy street by her cousin's home without asking an adult for permission. Her aunt is horrified. But Naima lives on a quiet street that she has permission to cross without asking. No one told her the rules were different at her aunt's.*

Often, children "misbehave" without intending to. How we respond to their behavior can influence how often and in what way they repeat that behavior. The toddler who spills his milk—either by accident or just to see how milk looks falling to the floor—will be influenced by the reaction he gets. If he gets a big, irritated reaction, he may use the same behavior again when attention is what he wants. Then the behavior becomes misbehavior. If the adult's reaction is low-key, the child doesn't get the message that this is a way to win attention. If he's handed a rag and asked to help clean up, he builds his belief that mistakes are okay and that he himself can help put things right.

How we react to unintentional "misbehavior" may determine whether that behavior will be repeated in the future as a way of achieving one of the four goals of misbehavior. We can learn to react in ways that encourage our children to seek belonging through constructive means.

At times, children "misbehave" because they are curious, tired, sick, hungry, bored, clumsy, or just trying to be helpful. The behavior we find troublesome may not really be misbehavior. We may simply have unrealistic expectations.

How we react may determine whether the behavior will be repeated as a way of achieving one of the four goals of misbehavior.

The Goals of Misbehavior[3]

A more in-depth look at Dreikurs's four goals of misbehavior can help us learn to recognize true misbehavior and understand the motives behind it.

Attention. All children need and deserve attention. Giving babies and young children attention is a major part of our task as parents. But attention becomes a goal of misbehavior when children believe they can belong *only* by demanding and getting attention.

> *Four-year-old Patti learns a new trick on the jungle gym and calls to her mom to watch. She is asking for appropriate attention. Her mother, who is sitting on a park bench reading, watches and says, "Patti, that looks hard. See what you can do by yourself! I'm glad you're having fun." She then continues reading while Patti practices her skills.*

Patti has asked for, and gotten, helpful attention. She feels she belongs both because her accomplishment has been recognized and because she enjoys physical activity, which she senses is appreciated.

*All children need and deserve attention. Attention becomes a goal of misbehavior when children believe they can belong **only** by demanding and getting attention.*

Attention would become a goal of misbehavior if Patti believed and acted as if she were worthwhile only when she kept her mother's attention. In this case, Patti might say, "Look at my new trick . . . now look again . . . do you like it? Watch my other tricks. Did you see that? Watch me do it again! . . . Mommy—watch!" If her mother tried to read, Patti would probably go on with her bids for attention. She might even fall off the jungle gym for a more dramatic dose of attention. This persistence would show Mother that Patti believed she belonged *only* by getting her mother's attention.

Power. Children want and seek power, as well as attention. A positive sense of power gives children a feeling of control over their environment, an important step in gaining independence. But power becomes a goal of misbehavior when children believe they belong *only* by being the boss.

> *Eighteen-month-old Al wants to feed himself. His parents support his desire for power in this area. They give Al a child-sized plate and spoon. They accept the fact that Al, his clothes, and the floor around him are messier because he feeds himself. From time to time, they recognize Al when he gets the food to his mouth with his spoon: "Al, look what you can do! You're feeding yourself!" Al is exercising power and strengthening his sense that he can belong through constructive behavior. Clearly, this sense is helped by his parents' reaction to his request for power.*

A positive sense of power gives children a feeling of control over their environment. Parents need to know how to share power appropriately so that power doesn't become a goal of misbehavior.

If Al's parents insisted on feeding him, Al might choose to struggle for power as a goal of misbehavior. Frustrated by not being able to feed himself, he might clamp his jaws shut and totally refuse to eat. Or he might demand his favorite bib and then his favorite cup. He might have to have his food arranged on his plate in a special way. He might insist on eating while standing up in his high chair. Al would probably push and push for more power, believing he belonged by being the one in charge. The meal might end with Al hurling his food across the room as a final way to say, "I'm the boss!" If his parents reacted to each demand either by giving in or by fighting with him, Al would be reinforced in believing that power is the only way to find a place.

Children definitely seek power. Parents need to know how to share power appropriately so that power doesn't become a goal of misbehavior.

Revenge. Children prefer to get attention in pleasant ways. But if they aren't successful in gaining positive attention, they will accept negative attention instead. They will often start a power struggle to further state their case of wanting to belong. If they lose the power struggle, they may choose the third goal of misbehavior—revenge. When children behave revengefully, they believe they can belong *only* by hurting others as they have been hurt.

> Every workday morning, Megan's father tries to get her dressed before taking the four-year-old to her child care provider. Because he wants to let Megan get as much sleep as possible, her father cuts dressing time to a minimum. Megan asks for attention by playing "catch me if you can." Her father chases her repeatedly, feeling annoyed and resentful. Getting some negative attention in this way only invites Megan to take power in the situation. She goes from playing chase to kicking and screaming as her father holds her to put her jacket on. A full-scale "I won't!"—"Oh, yes you will!" power struggle develops. Megan ends up being forced into her clothes and struggling as she is carried to the car.

> As her father greets the child care provider, Megan ups the ante. Megan hugs her child care provider and says, "I like you! I wish you were my daddy. My daddy's mean!" Belonging through revenge is complete. Megan's father goes off to work feeling hurt and angry.

The more sophisticated goal of revenge occurs as children move into the toddler and preschool years.

Although babies learn to misbehave at times to gain attention or power, children this young do not misbehave in order to get revenge. This more sophisticated emotional goal occurs as children move into the toddler and preschool years.

Display of inadequacy. The fourth goal of misbehavior is display of inadequacy. Like revenge, this goal is not pursued by infants, nor, in most cases, by toddlers. This is because displaying inadequacy is the response of children who have, over time, become completely discouraged in their search for belonging. Children with this goal believe they belong only by convincing others not to expect anything from them. They believe they are helpless. They give up and convince those around them to give up on them. Display of inadequacy doesn't appear overnight. It comes from months or years of discouragement at not finding a place through constructive means.

At a family gathering, five-year-old Bobby's uncle notices his nephew coloring. "Have you learned to write your name yet, Bobby?" he asks. "No," Bobby replies. "No?" asks his uncle in surprise. "Here, let me show you how." "No," answers Bobby, hanging his head. "I can't do it." "Hmm," says his uncle. "Well, what are you coloring?"

Wisely, Bobby's uncle has shifted his focus to something Bobby feels comfortable doing. This kind of encouragement can be the first step toward rebuilding Bobby's confidence about writing, so he'll be willing to try again in the future.

But why is Bobby discouraged about writing his name? When he was four, Bobby began learning to print the letters of his name. Like many young children, Bobby turned some of the letters around, and often his name on the page looked like "Boddy." Whenever Bobby wrote his name with backward *b*'s, his mother or father or older sister would say, "No, Bobby. That's not right. Those are *d*'s, not *b*'s." Over time, Bobby has become extremely discouraged about writing his name, and now he has given up.

Bobby's parents and sister were trying to help. But if they had changed their expectations, they might have handled this differently. Understanding that it is natural for children Bobby's age to write some letters backward, his family could have chosen to ignore the backward letters and simply say, "Look at how you're learning to write your name, Bobby! Is it fun?"

Identifying the Goals of Misbehavior

How do parents know when children are pursuing negative behavior goals? We suggest, with infants, that parents start from the assumption that the child is not *mis*behaving, but is behaving normally out of a specific need. A cranky, crying baby may be telling you that she is bored, hungry, tired, or feeling sick. She may need a little more gentle rocking or rubbing before she can fall asleep. While it's possible that an older baby may begin to seek power and attention inappropriately, it's more likely during the first year of life that she is simply using the communication ability she has to have her real needs met. If you believe her needs *are* being met, and troublesome behavior patterns continue, then your baby *may* be starting to pursue attention or power as a goal of misbehavior. If you do not respond immediately, it may be easier for you to identify what is wrong.

Display of inadequacy doesn't appear overnight. It comes from months or years of discouragement at not finding a place through constructive means.

As children get older, parents will find it easier to recognize true misbehavior and identify the goal. The key to identifying your child's goal is found in your own response to his or her behavior. To identify your child's goal, note carefully

- *how you feel* when the misbehavior happens
- *what you do* about the misbehavior
- *how your child responds* to what you do about the misbehavior

These three factors will help you determine the goal.

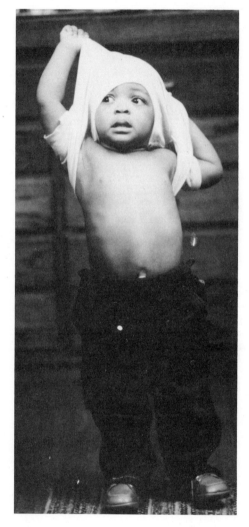

Attention. If your child has attention as her goal, you will probably feel *annoyed* and *remind or coax* her. In turn, she is likely to *temporarily stop the misbehavior,* having received the attention she was seeking. Later, the child may repeat the act for more attention or choose a different way to get your attention.

Power. The power-seeking child usually provokes you to *anger.* You feel your authority has been challenged. You in turn will either *try to make the child do what you want, or give in.* If you fight, he *fights back,* and you impress him with the value of power. If you give in, he *stops the misbehavior,* having gotten what he was after.

Revenge. A child who seeks revenge wants to get even, because she feels she has been wronged. Your likely response is to *feel emotionally hurt* by her attempt at revenge—also *physically hurt* if she's attacked you bodily. If you then get angry and *try to get even with the child,* she is likely to respond by *seeking more revenge.*

Remember that infants do not pursue the goal of revenge. Toddlers do seek revenge at times, but their behavior can also go out-of-bounds because they are upset or overstimulated.

Display of inadequacy. A child's display of inadequacy encourages you to *give up.* You *feel despair.* You *take no action* because you agree that the child isn't capable and you don't expect him to be able to perform the task. Therefore, *there is no improvement.*

The display of inadequacy *always* involves passive behavior—discouraged, the child does nothing. The other three goals may sometimes involve passive behavior. For example, a child may seek attention passively by simply expecting to be waited on (rather than actively, by shouting for attention). A child who stubbornly but silently refuses to budge when asked to get dressed or come to the table is taking a passive approach to pursuing power. Hateful stares may come from a wish for revenge.

Whether a child pursues a goal actively or passively, your clues to discovering the goal come from checking your feelings, the action you take, and your child's response to that action.

More About Misbehavior Goals

Children aren't always aware of the goals of their misbehavior. Also, children can change goals depending on how they see a situation.

Three-year-old Kevin clowns around at home to get attention. This gives him a sense of belonging. But at preschool with other children, Kevin's clowning around doesn't get him the attention he wants, so he begins to demand the teacher's attention more directly—by following her around, interrupting her when she's with another child, pushing to be first. Kevin's quest for attention at school is becoming a power struggle.

One type of behavior can be used for different goals. For example, a five-year-old may sit passively by, waiting for her father to tie her shoes, even though she already knows how. She's passively seeking attention. Another five-year-old may not tie his shoes—even though he has the skill—because he honestly believes he can't do it. This is a display of inadequacy.

Different behavior can also be used to achieve the same goal.

When two-year-old Laurie doesn't want to get into the car, she shows her power by crying. Later, when she doesn't want to go to bed, Laurie shows her power by challenging her parents and refusing to go.

Redirecting Children's Misbehavior

You don't *cause* your children to misbehave. Children aren't puppets: they make decisions based on the way they see things. However, you may reinforce children's misbehavior goals by responding in ways they have come to expect. By doing what a misbehaving child expects, you may unintentionally encourage him to continue the misbehavior because it pays off. For example, if you give your child attention—even for positive behavior—every time he wants it, he'll probably decide that he belongs only when he is the center of attention. He'll expect you to stop whatever you're doing and attend to him. If he doesn't get a pleasant response from you, he'll accept an unpleasant one—as long as he gets the attention he seeks.

Following are some general guidelines for dealing with misbehavior according to its goal. These general guidelines are based on doing the

If you do the opposite of what your child expects, you won't reinforce her goals.

unexpected.[4] If you do the opposite of what your child expects, you won't reinforce her goal. This may influence her to change her perception. She gets no payoff for the misbehavior. Challenging as it may be, changing your response involves changing both your behavior *and* your feelings.

Attention. When possible, ignore misbehavior that seeks attention. Refuse to be annoyed. Avoid always giving attention when the child is asking for it. Be sure to give positive attention when your child is not expecting it.

> *Three-year-old Karen often seeks her parents' attention by making noise while they watch the evening news on television. Over time, Karen's parents have learned to ignore Karen's noise, or, when necessary, remove Karen from the living room and have her play by herself in her room during this half-hour.*

While they've been working on this problem, Karen's parents have also made a point of noticing Karen at times when she isn't seeking attention.

> *Entering the living room one night, Karen's mother found her husband reading the paper, with Karen curled up beside him paging happily through a picture book. Her mother said, "Karen, it's so nice to see you reading quietly next to Daddy." Later that evening, when Karen had finished looking at her picture book, Mother said to her, "Why don't you get that book you were looking at and we can read it together now?" Karen is learning that she deserves and will receive attention from her parents, but not on demand!*

Power. Withdraw from the conflict by refusing to fight or give in—don't let yourself become angry. If possible, let the child experience the consequences of the misbehavior.

> *When two-year-old Todd refused to eat his lunch, his dad used to trick, argue, and finally try to force his son to eat by refusing to let him down from his high chair. Lately, Dad has been trying a different approach. First of all, he has cut down the size of Todd's morning snack. Then, at lunch, after giving Todd a reasonable variety of food and several minutes to decide to eat, he simply lifts his son down from the high chair. "I guess you're not hungry," he says. "Maybe you'll feel more like eating at suppertime." Todd's dad offers only juice*

for Todd's afternoon snack, and then provides a balanced meal at suppertime. Todd is learning that his refusal to eat won't provoke a power struggle anymore. Instead, he has had to live with the consequences of not eating. Already Todd's behavior at lunch has improved.

Revenge. When your child is after revenge, it isn't easy to keep from feeling hurt. But the cycle of revenge can begin to subside only when you avoid feeling hurt—difficult as that may be. Instead of trying to get even, work to build trust and mutual respect.

Four-year-old Clara's parents have recently separated. Lately, when Mother goes to put Clara to bed, her daughter stands firm, pushes out her lower lip, and says, "No! I don't want you—I want Daddy!" Mother feels very hurt, but she knows a hurt or angry response won't help Clara cope. So Mother tells Clara, "I know you miss Daddy. When you visit him this weekend, then he can put you to bed." By being respectful, Mother is letting Clara know that she understands her daughter's feelings. Over time, this will help Clara learn that she doesn't have to misbehave in order to deal with her feelings.

Display of inadequacy. Remember that children who display inadequacy are extremely discouraged. It's important not to give up on such a child! Avoid criticism. Find any area of strength to encourage. Focus on the child's slightest effort or improvement.

Marty, who is five, has decided he will never learn to ride a bike. When his friends ride trikes and bikes at the local park, he doesn't even want to bring his tricycle along. Instead, he sits on the swing by himself. Wisely, Marty's grandmother says nothing about riding. Instead, she's beginning to look for things Marty does well. "You really know how to pump high on the swing, Marty!" she exclaims. "Can you show me how?" This kind of encouragement, over time, can show Marty that he is capable of many things. This in turn may eventually help him find the courage to try to ride a bicycle. Patience and encouragement will go a long way toward helping Marty build confidence in himself.

The Flip Side: Positive Behavior Goals

As parents work to redirect misbehavior, it can be helpful to consider what *positive* goal to encourage instead. Children who want *attention* may also want to be involved. Encouraging helpfulness and social interest can help refocus that drive for attention in a way that is useful to both the child and others. Positive *power* means being responsible for one's own behavior and decisions. If you're involved in power struggles with your child, look for ways to build a sense of independence and capability.

Surprisingly, *revenge,* too, can be turned in a more useful direction. Children who seek revenge often have a strong desire for justice and fairness. Guiding such children to play and share equally encourages this.

Even aspects of a *display of inadequacy* can be refocused in a more positive direction. For example, displaying inadequacy involves withdrawal, and it's important for children to learn appropriate times to show courage by withdrawing from conflict or dangerous situations. While working to build a discouraged child's positive feelings about himself, parents can also help the child learn to recognize when to withdraw or stand on the sidelines.

It's important to keep in mind that troublesome behavior may or may not be "misbehavior." Too, when our children do misbehave, they are not usually aware of the goals of their behavior. However, they *are* aware of our reactions to how they behave. In the next few chapters, we'll take a broader look at helpful ways to respond—ways to talk with, listen to, and guide children so they develop positive beliefs about themselves and their place in the world.

Notes

1. Alfred Adler, *The Science of Living* (Garden City, N.Y.: Anchor Books, 1969), p. 4.

2. Rudolf Dreikurs and Vickie Soltz, *Children: The Challenge* (New York: Hawthorn Books, 1964), pp. 57-63.

3. For a more in-depth discussion of the four goals of misbehavior, see Don Dinkmeyer and Gary D. McKay, *Systematic Training for Effective Parenting (STEP): The Parent's Handbook,* 3d ed. (Circle Pines, Minn.: American Guidance Service, 1989).

4. Dreikurs and Soltz, p. 181.

Activity for the Week

Observe your child's behavior.
- Is the behavior due to the child's developmental level or experience?
- Is the behavior actually misbehavior? If so, use the following steps to identify the goal:

1. Describe specifically what your child did.
2. Identify your feelings and what you did about the misbehavior.
3. Describe how your child responded to what you did.
4. Based on your feelings and your child's response, decide if your child's goal of misbehavior was attention, power, revenge, or display of inadequacy.

Consider how you might change your response and begin to redirect the misbehavior. Also, look for opportunities to help your child develop positive goals.

Goals of Misbehavior

With babies, start from the assumption that the child does not have a goal of *misbehavior*, but is behaving normally out of a specific need. The concept of *goals* has limited application to infants, and only in the areas of attention and power. While it's possible that an older baby may seek attention or power through misbehavior, it's more likely during the first year of life that the baby is simply using the communication skills she or he has to get real needs met. Babies do not pursue revenge or display of inadequacy.

Toddlers are not likely to display inadequacy, since this goal comes after years of discouragement.

The following examples are just possibilities. The goal depends on how the parent feels, what the parent does, and how the child responds to the parent's action.

TODDLERS

Belief	Goal	Parent's Reaction	Child's Response to Parent's Reaction	Age Level Behavior	Alternatives for Parents
I need to be noticed.	Attention	Annoyance. Tendency to remind child to stop.	Temporarily stops misbehavior. Later resumes behavior or disturbs in similar or other way.	Whines.	Give attention for positive behavior. Redirect child to more appropriate activity.
You can't make me.	Power	Anger, exasperation. Tendency to fight or give in.	Intensifies misbehavior or submits with defiance.	Answers request for cooperation with immediate "NO!"	Give choices so child can make decision.
You don't love me!	Revenge	Deep hurt. Tendency to get even.	Seeks more revenge by intensifying misbehavior or choosing another weapon.	Hits or calls parent name when doesn't get own way.	Avoid feeling emotionally hurt and punishing child. Build trust and mutual respect.

PRESCHOOLERS

Belief	Goal	Parent's Reaction	Child's Response to Parent's Reaction	Age Level Behavior	Alternatives for Parents
I want to be noticed or served.	Attention	Annoyance. Tendency to remind child to stop.	Temporarily stops misbehavior. Later resumes behavior or disturbs in similar or other way.	"Watch me now!" Seeks constant parent contact.	Give attention for positive behavior when child is not making bid for it. Set aside some time each day to give full attention to child.
I am in control. You can't make me!	Power	Anger, exasperation. Tendency to fight or give in.	Intensifies misbehavior or submits with defiance.	Has temper tantrums. Resists directions.	Withdraw from power struggle. Don't give in just to make peace. Let consequence occur.
You don't love me!	Revenge	Deep hurt. Tendency to get even.	Seeks more revenge by intensifying misbehavior or choosing another weapon.	Screams, yells, "I hate you, Mommy," "I don't love you anymore!"	Avoid feeling hurt and punishing child. Build trust and mutual respect.
I am helpless. I can't.	Display of inadequacy	Despair, hopelessness. Tendency to agree with child that nothing can be done.	Responds passively or fails to respond to whatever is done. Refuses to try and shows no improvement.	Whines, cries, "I can't do it!"	Encourage *any* efforts or attempts. Don't pity.

Positive Goals of Behavior

Babies are in the process of *beginning* to develop positive goals. They are learning to get some needs met through attention and power, and are also learning to be involved and to contribute as they coo, play, and cuddle with parents.

These examples are just possibilities. There are no specific parent reactions to these goals. The parent just feels good about what is happening.

TODDLERS

Belief	Goal	Behavior	How Parents Can Encourage
I want to be like others.	Attention Involvement Contribution	Imitates parent sweeping, cooking, doing other chores.	Recognize and let child know you appreciate the help.
I can do it my way.	Power Independence	Wants to feed and undress self.	Let child do as much as possible for self.
It's mine!	Justice Fairness Social interest	Learns to respect another child's toy.	Encourage child to share toy when done playing with it.
I want to be reassured.	Withdrawal from conflict Conflict resolution	Wants to be held and comforted.	Hold and reassure child. Let child know it's okay to be angry.

PRESCHOOLERS

Belief	Goal	Behavior	How Parents Can Encourage
I belong when I contribute.	Attention Involvement Contribution	Starts to clear dishes from table after meal.	Recognize and let child know you appreciate the help.
I'm able to make my own decisions. I can do it!	Power Independence	Picks out clothes to wear.	Encourage child's initiative.
I want to cooperate and get along with others.	Justice Fairness Social interest	Shares toys rather than fights over them.	Show that you appreciate child's effort to cooperate.
I can handle conflict in an acceptable way.	Withdrawal from conflict Control of physical impulses (biting, hitting, pushing, kicking)	Verbally communicates feelings to others rather than physically showing feelings.	Model conflict resolution with child using words rather than physical means.

41

Points to Remember

1. Starting in infancy, we develop our lifestyle—beliefs about who we are, who other people are, what is important in life, and how to act so we can belong.

2. Five major factors influence the development of lifestyle:
   - heredity
   - family atmosphere and values
   - role models
   - methods of parenting
   - position in the family—actual and psychological

3. Behavior reflects lifestyle beliefs. Most behavior has a social purpose—to find a place, *to belong.*

4. Children discover they get a feeling of belonging from the responses of others. They learn to get responses by cooperative or uncooperative behavior.

5. Sometimes behavior that troubles us is due to our faulty expectations. When children's actions stem from curiosity, tiredness, illness, hunger, boredom, or attempts to be helpful, this is not misbehavior.

6. There are four goals of misbehavior:
   - attention
   - power
   - revenge
   - display of inadequacy

7. To identify the goal of misbehavior, notice
   - how you feel when your child misbehaves
   - what you do about it
   - how your child responds to what you do

8. Children usually aren't aware of the goal of their misbehavior.

9. When your infant or baby's behavior troubles you, start from the assumption that the child is not *mis*behaving, but has a specific need.

10. Infants do not misbehave for revenge or to display inadequacy. Toddlers rarely display inadequacy.

11. When your child misbehaves, do the opposite of what he expects. Give positive attention and power; work to build trust and self-confidence.

Just for You

What's Your Priority?

Although each lifestyle is unique, all lifestyles contain four *personality priorities,* or themes:
- to feel superior (superiority)
- to feel in control of things (control)
- to please others (pleasing)
- to be comfortable (comfort)

Everyone seeks a feeling of belonging through these four priorities. But most of us, for our own sense of belonging, put a higher value on one or two of the priorities.

You can find out which priorities you value the most by a simple test. Priorities are related to what a person most wants to avoid. Which of the following situations would you *most* want to avoid? Put a *1* before it. Decide which situation would be second to avoid, and put a *2* before it. Rank the others *3* and *4.*

_____ being rejected
_____ being humiliated
_____ being under stress or in conflict
_____ being unproductive

If you most want to avoid "being rejected," *pleasing* is your highest priority. (You want to please to avoid rejection.)

If you most want to avoid "being humiliated," *control* is your highest priority. (You don't want to be controlled by someone else.)

If you most want to avoid "being under stress or in conflict," *comfort* is your highest priority. (You don't want stress or conflict to disturb you.)

If you most want to avoid "being unproductive," *superiority* is your highest priority. (You want to have meaning in your life.)

Now you can see how you value the four priorities.

The following chart lists some of the ways the different priorities can affect you and your children.

Continued on next page.

Priority	How Others May Feel	Price You Pay for Your Priority	What You Most Want to Avoid	Possible Negative Results for Children	Possible Positive Results for Children
Superiority	Inadequate	Being overburdened, overresponsible	Unproductivity, meaninglessness	Feeling inadequate or having to be perfect	Being creative, having a positive outlook on life
Control	Challenged	Inability to get close to people	Humiliation, the unexpected	Facing power contests—being afraid to share feelings	Learning limits and organization
Pleasing	Pleased at first, then perhaps disgusted	Being taken advantage of, disrespected	Rejection	Learning to be disrespectful and take advantage	Having less conflict, being understood
Comfort	Annoyed or irritated	Lack of accomplishment	Stress or conflict	Having their interests go unrecognized or seem unimportant	Having less conflict, being able to pursue own interests

- How does your use of a priority affect your life and your approach to parenting?
- What changes might you want to make?
- What will you do this week with what you've learned about yourself?

To learn more about the personality priorities, read *The Effective Parent* by Don Dinkmeyer et al. (Circle Pines, Minn.: American Guidance Service, 1987); *Out of Apples* by Lee Schnebly (Tucson, Ariz.: Manzanas Press, 1984—write to Manzanas Press, 2641 N. Arcadia, Tucson, AZ 85712); and *The Pleasers* by Kevin Leman (Old Tappan, N.J.: Fleming Revell, 1987). Or listen to the audiocassette *Lifestyle Interpretation* by Roy Kern (Coral Springs, Fla.: CMTI Press, 1982—write to CMTI Press, Box 8268, Coral Springs, FL 33065).

CHAPTER 3

Building Self-Esteem in the Early Years

It will be easier for children to form positive beliefs about themselves and to find their places in the world if they have strong self-esteem. Self-esteem is a positive view of oneself. It is an attitude we develop when we are loved and we know we are lovable and capable. When we have healthy self-esteem, we have a positive self-image—we value ourselves.

With high self-esteem, we accept ourselves and our feelings. Children who feel good about themselves are better able to deal with the world. Self-esteem is the main factor that prepares every child for successes and failures as a human being.[1] Our feelings of self-worth are beliefs that form the basis of our personality and determine how we use our abilities. When we believe we are valuable, lovable, and worthwhile, we are more ready to meet life's challenges.

Birth to age six is an ideal period for the development of self-esteem. Children are forming beliefs about their own self-worth based on their perception of the responses they get. It is the time when parents are in the best position to strengthen their children's sense of self-worth. So how do we go about it?

Children who feel good about themselves are better able to deal with the world.

Begin with Respect

One way to help build children's self-esteem is to base your relationships with them on mutual respect. Mutual respect means believing and behaving as if both parent and child are unconditionally valuable. You treat your child with respect. You expect your child to treat you—and others—with respect.

Respect Yourself

For your child to treat you with respect, it's first important that you respect yourself. Your healthy self-esteem is the model for your children. When you value, appreciate, and accept yourself as you are, you are a positive role model.

There are a number of ways to build and maintain self-respect. It will be helpful for you to work to
- develop your own interests, goals, and strengths
- recognize your efforts, rather than focusing only on results

- be positive about yourself and others
- use your sense of humor to keep things in perspective
- realize that you'll make mistakes, but that your children will probably survive anyway
- take time for yourself, to renew your strength and patience
- remember that you are worthwhile simply because you are human, not because you are a successful parent[2]

*Four-year-old Mandy breaks her new red crayon the first time she uses it. She lets out a howl. Red is her favorite color, and she wanted to keep all the tips sharp. At the same time, her mom breaks a pipe she is trying to repair under the sink. **She** lets out a howl. She wanted to save money. Now she'll have to spend money, and she's also got a mess on her hands. Believing in mutual respect, Mom says to Mandy, "Things are breaking for both of us. I feel upset and angry. I'll bet you do, too!"*

From an adult point of view, a broken pipe is a lot more serious than a broken crayon. But from a child's point of view, they might be equally tragic. Mom has shown that Mandy's concerns are important. She has also demonstrated her own self-esteem. She didn't put down either herself or Mandy for what happened to each of them. If Mandy continues to receive respect and see models of self-esteem, she is likely to learn to respect herself and others.

Help Children Learn Mutual Respect

Babies and young children do not naturally show respect for others. In fact, *it is normal and healthy for them to be self-centered.* We can't expect any young child to be as respectful as an adult is capable of being. But young children are capable of *learning* mutual respect if they are treated respectfully.

It is never too early to begin sowing the seeds of mutual respect.

It is never too early to begin sowing the seeds of mutual respect. To do this:
- Show young children you love and value them by giving their feelings consideration. "You're mad that Kitty won't play, aren't you? She wants to go sleep now." "Look at that smile! I'm glad to see you, too!" "I know you feel sad about losing your teddy bear. Let's talk about it."
- Appreciate their uniqueness. "What a loud, happy voice I hear coming from your crib! You like to talk, don't you?" "Your hand is

just the right size to reach behind the dresser. Can you find the ball that rolled under there?" "You draw such pretty flowers! Let's make this picture into a card to send to Grandma!"

- Find ways to support their interests. "You like to build things. Let's make something with your blocks." "I know you like Curious George. We can get another book about him at the library."
- Give them reasonable control over their lives where possible. "Sounds like you're hungry! Let's warm up your bottle so you can eat." "Would you like to wear the green shirt or the yellow shirt today?"
- Let them see that mistakes can be viewed as feedback and are not to be feared. "I didn't use enough flour in these cookies—see how flat they are? Next time, I'll know how much flour to use." "Your glass of milk got knocked off the table. Next time, you'll know not to set it so close to the edge."
- And remember to show respect for yourself. "I fixed the broken door the best I could. I'm glad it works better now." "I had a nice long walk—that helped me feel good today!"

Encouragement—The Key Ingredient

Mutual respect provides the foundation for children's self-respect. Parents can use the skill of *encouragement* to help build on this foundation. Respect is an attitude we can model and teach; *encouragement* is a *skill* we can learn and use to help children grow in self-esteem.

Encouragement is a skill we can learn and use to help children grow in self-esteem.

Encouragement helps children develop positive attitudes and beliefs about themselves by focusing on their strengths and assets. When we encourage children, we accept *them,* even though we don't always accept their behavior.

With encouragement, we recognize effort and improvement—rather than expect or demand perfection. When parents encourage, they take the focus off comparing children. Comparisons can lead children to believe that their worth depends on being better than others. With encouragement, parents can instead help each child appreciate his or her own unique individual qualities.

> *Corey and Anders are eleven-month-old cousins. They look alike, but they act very differently. At any family gathering, Corey is constantly moving. Whatever catches his eye, he wants to investigate. He is lightning quick and very*

determined. Anders, on the other hand, sits and smiles and babbles. If he has a toy to chew on, he's content.

The families of Corey and Anders want to encourage both boys. They do this by appreciating each one. The strengths of both styles are recognized. The differences are clear, but no negative comparisons are made. They say to each child, "You sure look like you're having fun."

When we encourage our children, we let them make an *internal* evaluation—we let them decide for themselves if they are pleased with their efforts. They don't depend on pleasing others to feel good about their efforts.

*Five-year-old Lai is learning to print. She brings her work to her dad and says, "What do you think? Did I do a good job? Is it good enough?" As a dad who believes in encouragement, he answers, "What **you** think about your printing is most important. Do you like the letters you've made? I can see you're working hard and you seem to be enjoying yourself."*

This response might sound a bit unnatural, but it is an encouraging one. It stresses self-evaluation by guiding Lai to make her own decisions about her work. It invites her to take responsibility for herself, rather than to depend on pleasing another for her satisfaction.

How Do Parents Encourage?

Parents who are encouraging aid their children in developing inner resources and courage. They help their children find ways to handle challenges. Parents do this in several ways:

- By valuing and accepting children as they are. Children have different abilities, interests, and rates of development. They also have ups and downs that are reflected in their moods and behavior. Each child, too, has her or his own strengths and weaknesses. By appreciating and accepting *both,* parents show children they are valued just as they are.
- By believing in children, and showing it. "Go ahead—you can reach the ball by yourself." "I know you're excited, but you can wait ten more minutes for the party to start." "You'll learn to tie your shoelaces."
- By treating children with respect. Remember, mutual respect and self-respect go hand in hand.

- By making it clear a child's worth doesn't depend on being better than others. Judgments and comparisons are not encouraging. An encouraged child believes in his or her own value.
- By appreciating children's efforts and improvements. "You're getting better at remembering to wash your hands before supper." "Look at that! You got the spoon to your mouth!"
- By appreciating children's strengths and positive qualities. "It was nice of you to share your toys with your cousins. Did you have fun together?" "Maybe if you sing to your baby brother, he'll have an easier time falling asleep. He likes to hear you sing."
- By showing real interest in areas that interest children (and not only the areas *parents* feel are important).
- By keeping a sense of humor. A sense of humor shows your child how to keep mistakes in perspective. This can help both you and your child relax. It can help you encourage *yourself,* too!

A sense of humor shows your child how to keep mistakes in perspective.

The Difference Between Encouragement and Praise

In their efforts to build children's self-esteem, parents sometimes confuse encouragement with praise. But praise and encouragement are not the same thing. Each has a different purpose.

Praise is a type of reward. It is based on competition and comparison. Praise from a parent gives a child the reward of being valued by the parent. It is given when a child has accomplished something.

Encouragement is given for effort or improvement. It isn't based on competition or comparison, but on a child's assets and strengths. Encouragement from a parent helps a child accept himself and feel worthy. It raises his self-esteem. It can be given at any time, even when a child feels he isn't doing well or is facing failure.

> *Eva shows her mom a picture she's painted. The four-year-old's mother isn't sure exactly what the drawing is supposed to show. But she quickly tells Eva, "This is a wonderful picture! You did a great job on it! I'm very proud of you!"*

Eva may be happy with her mother's enthusiastic response. But Eva may also be learning that it is important to please *others.* After a number of such praise responses, she may start to believe that what others think of her decides her worth. She may start to fear the times when her mother doesn't give as much praise.

Three-year-old Luke smilingly brings his stepfather a sample of his crayon artwork. His stepfather looks at it carefully. Then he says to Luke, "I can tell you're happy with your picture. I see you like to use red and green."

Praise and encouragement are not the same thing. Encouragement helps a child become self-motivated. Praise teaches a child to please others.

Luke's stepfather is encouraging Luke to appreciate his own efforts. He wants the boy to learn to make his own judgments rather than rely on his stepfather to decide if he is worthy. Luke's stepdad could also ask Luke to tell him about the picture first, giving Luke a chance to share his ideas and feelings about it.

Encouragement helps a child become self-motivated. Praise teaches a child to please others. While there is nothing wrong with wanting to please someone, there is a problem when a child believes she *must*

please in order to feel worthwhile. Praise should be used *with* encouragement and *to* encourage. If you accept your child and are proud just because she is your child, then praise can be encouraging.

> *Two-and-a-half-year-old Leah has gotten through her first full day of using the toilet with no accidents in between. At bedtime her father tells her, "Good for you, Leah! You used the potty every time today!" Leah beams happily. She feels good inside about her accomplishment. This is because her family has noticed her efforts and strides in toilet training from the beginning. When she first used the toilet successfully, they smiled and asked her, "Did you like using the potty like Mommy and Daddy?" When she wet her pants, no one made an issue of it. Instead, her mother said, "Looks like you need some dry pants. Why don't you go get them from your drawer, and I'll help you clean up."*

This kind of encouragement, over weeks and months, has helped Leah make a successful transition to using the toilet—at her own speed. Her father's words of praise tonight are encouraging because Leah knows she is accepted and loved regardless of when or how well she succeeds in using the toilet.

The Language of Encouragement

Although there are times when praise can be encouraging, parents will be most effective if they avoid praising children too often. Remember, we encourage to help our children believe in *themselves*. But when we use words such as *good*, *great*, and *excellent*, we're usually not doing that. Instead, we're expressing *our* values and opinions.

Encouragement has its own language. Here are some examples of phrases that express encouragement for young children's efforts:

"You seem to like that."
"How do you feel about it?"
"You can do it."
"Thanks; that helped me a lot."
"I need your help on _____."
"You really worked hard on that!"
"You're getting better at _____." (Be specific.)

Encouraging Learning—Without Praise or Pressure

You are your child's first teacher. You want your child to learn how to face changes and challenges. You want her to develop skills and a positive attitude toward learning. Your child has a better chance of doing so if you are more interested in her *learning how to learn* than in her performing well.

Here are some guidelines for encouraging learning:

1. Provide a learning environment and learning experiences. Give your baby lots of space to crawl and explore safely. Let your toddler scribble, paint, and build. Allow your preschooler opportunities to play with other children.

2. Follow your child's interest. If your child loves elephants, find books about them. Ask him to tell you stories about them.

3. Watch for chances for learning. On a trip to the park, point out animals and flowers or talk with your child about what people are doing.

Look for ways to support your child's interests.

4. Ask open-ended questions. Questions that have no simple, single answer encourage your child to think, explain, and explore. "What do you think the squirrel will do with that acorn?" "How did you make your block tower so tall?"

5. Recognize and encourage. "You did that all by yourself! You're happy you can button your shirt."

6. Accept your child's feelings of failure and encourage more attempts. "Oops—you dropped the ball. That's okay. Let's try again."

7. Make learning fun. Make games out of learning to count, dress, or climb stairs.

8. Help your child see the alternatives in challenging situations. "I know you're scared of the thunder. Let's look at this book about storms—maybe we'll find out why they're so noisy!" "It's hard to pick up all these toys at once! Why don't you start with putting the trucks in the cupboard . . . *(when finished with first task)* . . . No more trucks? That was quick! What part can you pick up next?"

We want to encourage our children to learn—not push them. Many parents want their children to be prepared as early as possible to reach high goals in education and to compete in sports. So they push their children hard and fast. But children pay a price for such pressure. They may become anxious about how they perform. They may get headaches and stomachaches or have other physical problems if they fail to please. They may resist the pushing and constantly fight their parents.[3] We encourage learning by setting reasonable goals with the child, accepting her efforts, and appreciating her improvements.

Chart 3, "Encouragement vs. Pressure," illustrates additional differences between encouraging learning and pushing children to learn.

Communicating Love

When children know they are loved, they believe they are lovable. This helps develop their self-esteem. Giving mutual respect and encouragement are clear ways we communicate to our children that we love them. Here are some additional ways to say "I love you."

1. Tell them so, clearly and directly. Give the message every day, to every child: "Good morning, Tommy. I love you." "Guess who loves you as big as a mountain? Guess who loves you as high as the moon?" "Let's name all the people in your life who love you: Grandpa, Tracy, Aunt Carol . . ."

We want to encourage our children to learn— not push them.

For babies and young children, love communicated by touch is more powerful than any words.

2. Show appreciation. "Good night, Elizabeth. I liked my day with you. I'll be happy to see you when you wake up." "Miguel, you're such a snuggly snuggler! It's fun to snuggle with you." "Oh my, you're getting big! I love to watch you grow and learn."

3. Show love through touch. For babies and young children, love communicated by touch is more powerful than any words. The physical care of babies demands a lot of body contact. The way we hold and caress our babies as we bathe, dress, change, and feed them can very clearly tell them they are cared for.

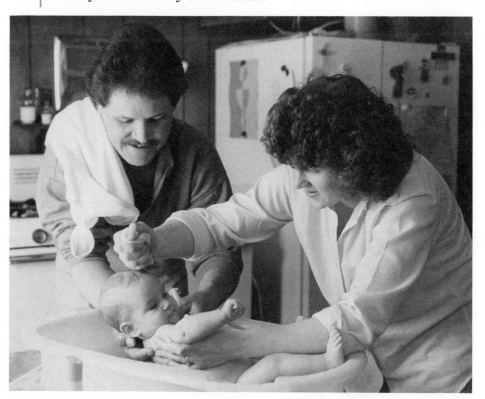

As our children move through toddlerhood and the preschool years, they often push away from our affection. Yet they still need to be told through touch that they are loved. We have many chances for touch every day as we help them dress themselves, as we teach them how to wash, as we tuck them in at night. Gentle, caring touch clearly says, "I love you."

There will be times when they say, "No, I don't want a hug." That's okay—we can respect their feelings. But there will be more times when climbing onto our laps for a moment of quiet reassurance is just what they want. Also, we can play physical games of "chase" and "wrestling" with them. Young children delight in bouncing, rolling, falling, and bumping together. Love is communicated through both enthusiastic touch and gentle touch.

4. Spend focused time with each child. We can spend all day with our children and not spend a focused moment. By *focused time,* we mean a time when you put aside all other concerns and give your entire attention. Do an activity you and your child both enjoy—and be sure your child helps choose the activity most of the time. This might mean scheduling time or making use of an opportunity as it occurs. In our pressured, grown-up world, finding time to do this can be challenging. However, the reward makes it worth it. When we choose to give our children focused time on a regular basis, our children get the message that they are important.

5. Guide behavior with respect. It's hard to overstate the importance of respect! Our positive efforts to communicate love can easily be undone by expressions of displeasure with our children. What we say and do when our children make mistakes or misbehave is very important to their sense of being loved and their self-esteem.

In our pressured, grown-up world, finding time for our children can be challenging. The rewards make it worth it.

A Word About Neglect and Abuse

The right words and touches communicate love to children. If loving words and touches are seldom or never given, a form of abuse takes place—psychological neglect. The wrong words and touches communicate the lack of love. The wrong touches (violent, sexual) are physical abuse. The wrong words (insulting, constantly critical) are verbal abuse.

If a parent continually feels hostile, hurtful, or intensely angry toward a child—or worries about acting on such feelings—the parent needs to seek professional help. A doctor, member of the clergy, or crisis-intervention center will be able to direct the parent to someone who can help. Parents can also check the phone book under *crisis intervention* or *Parents Anonymous.*

Encouragement Away from Home— Choosing Child Care

Whether your children are with you or in the care of someone else, you want them to be consistently treated with love and respect, to be encouraged, and to have their self-esteem built up. For various reasons, most parents need to have their children cared for outside of the home at least some of the time. Working parents—married or single—need child care. Parents at home during the day need it to give themselves time away from their children to renew their own energy, to pursue other interests, and to be with other adults. Some parents look for child care or a preschool so their children will have a chance to be with other children.

Here are some types of child care arrangements you might explore for your child. The type of setting you choose will depend on your child's needs. (For example: Would your child be happier in a home setting with just a few other children, or in a preschool where there may be opportunities to interact with more children of the same age?) It will also depend on your family circumstances, your work schedule, and finances or financial assistance available to you.

- Arrange for a friend or relative to care for your child.
- Hire a child care provider to come into your home.
- Enroll your child in a family day care home, child care center, or preschool.
- Form a co-op with other parents to share care of several neighborhood children. Co-ops may be formed through established neighborhood organizations or church groups, or by talking to individual neighbors.[4]

You'll want to be sure that the person or center you choose has a philosophy of child care similar to yours. When selecting child care, keep the following questions in mind:

- What are your state's licensing requirements? Almost all states require both child care centers and family day care homes to be licensed or registered. Licensing generally assures a minimum standard of safety, though it does not necessarily guarantee a quality program. You'll want to make this judgment as the parent of your child.
- How many children are there for each adult? Most states set their own limits, but the National Association for the Education of Young Children recommends one adult for every three infants, six toddlers, or ten preschoolers. Most states do not regulate group size, but research shows that smaller groups are better for children.
- Is the home or center safe? Is the caregiver reliable and consistent? What are the caregiver's qualifications and experience with children your child's age?
- Is a variety of interesting toys and materials available to children of different ages? Are there activities that encourage social development? Do the children seem happy and involved? Be alert for situations where the television is used to keep the children occupied.

Before your toddler or preschooler enters any child care situation, talk to her about it, listen to her feelings, and answer all her questions.

- In a center or preschool, do the teachers encourage learning and development *without pressuring* children?
- How much parent involvement is expected or encouraged? Parents should be able to visit the program at any time once a child is enrolled, without an appointment.

Before making your final selection, visit the home or center several times (at various times of the day). Get to know the caregivers or teachers. Do you agree on discipline? Daily routines? Important values? Talk to other parents, too.

Before your toddler or preschooler enters any child care situation, talk to him about it, listen to his feelings, and answer all his questions. Take him for a visit so he can meet the caregivers, teachers, and other children before being enrolled.[5]

Have the Courage to Be Imperfect

As you read and think about the challenges of building your child's self-esteem, learning to encourage, and making important choices about child care and early learning, it's easy to feel overwhelmed. You may be wondering, "How can I possibly do all this? And what if I make a mistake?"

It may help if you remind yourself that you can't *always* show respect or be a constant model of encouragement—no one can! And, like all parents, you will make mistakes in your choices and decisions about raising your children. What you *can* do is keep in mind a general attitude of mutual respect, make an effort to encourage as much as you can, and have *the courage to be imperfect.*[6] When you develop the courage to be imperfect, you accept yourself as you are, without any need to be mistake-free or to focus on your child's mistakes. You don't fear mistakes. If you have the courage to be imperfect, you can concentrate on the present, not worry about the past.

We have discussed how important it is to help children develop self-esteem. But it's also important for parents themselves to have strong self-esteem. Parenting is a challenging task. Neither you nor your children will always handle behavior and emotions exactly "right."

You need to encourage *yourself.* Recognize what you are doing well. Focus on what helps you feel good about yourself. Above all, work to grow in the courage to be imperfect. Courageous parents
- see challenges, rather than problems
- get satisfaction from doing their best, not from any outside evaluation or from results
- consider what to do in a difficult situation, rather than just think it is hopeless
- accept that they will make mistakes—there are no "perfect" parents
- believe they will succeed if they go on trying

Parents with strong self-esteem help their children develop strong self-esteem. Children who see their parents face life's challenges with courage will develop the courage to do the same.

Notes

1. Dorothy Corkille Briggs, *Your Child's Self-Esteem: The Key to Life* (New York: Doubleday, Dolphin Books, 1975), p. 3.

2. This topic is treated in more depth in Don Dinkmeyer et al., *Systematic Training for Effective Parenting (STEP): The Effective Parent* (Circle Pines, Minn.: American Guidance Service, 1987), pp. 31-37.

3. For further discussion, read David Elkind, *Miseducation: Preschoolers at Risk* (New York: Knopf, 1987) and *The Hurried Child: Growing Up Too Fast Too Soon* (Reading, Mass.: Addison-Wesley, 1981).

4. Helen Neville and Mona Halaby, *No-Fault Parenting* (Tucson, Ariz.: The Body Press, 1984), pp. 331-32, 334.

5. For additional information about choosing child care, see Sue Bredekamp, ed., *Developmentally Appropriate Practice in Early Childhood Programs Serving Children from Birth Through Age 8* (Washington, D.C.: National Association for the Education of Young Children, 1987); Laura L. Dittman, "Finding the Best Care for Your Infant or Toddler" (Washington, D.C.: National Center for Clinical Infant Programs and the National Association for the Education of Young Children, 1985); and Gwen Morgan, *The National State of Child Care Regulation 1986* (Watertown, Mass.: Work/Family Directions, Inc., 1987).

6. The concept of The Courage to Be Imperfect was originally developed by Dr. Rudolf Dreikurs, an internationally known author and psychiatrist.

Activity for the Week

Practice encouraging your children and yourself.
- Find specific ways to encourage your children. Observe the results of your efforts.
- Focus on your own strengths, efforts, and improvements. Continue to use the self-affirming statements from the "Just for You" section of Chapter 1.

Chart 3

Encouragement vs. Pressure

	Encouragement	Pressure
Infants	Allowing infant to explore surroundings at own pace.	Overstimulating or forcing stimulation infant not ready for. Introducing infant to animal when clearly afraid.
	Giving infant age-appropriate toys.	Giving infant toys beyond age or ability level.
	Allowing infant to develop at own physical rate.	Coaxing infant to crawl or walk before physically capable.
	Helping infant give up breast or bottle when she shows interest in using cup.	Forcing infant to give up breast or bottle before ready.
Toddlers	Supporting toddler in beginning toilet training when he shows interest and physical ability to control bodily functions.	Forcing toddler to use potty or begin toilet training before he shows interest or is physically capable.
	Helping toddler give up pacifier, blanket, or security object when he shows interest in doing so.	Removing security object when still emotionally dependent on it.
	Guiding toddler to display age-appropriate behavior, such as trying to use eating utensils, in social situations.	Demanding that toddler behave more maturely.
Preschoolers	Encouraging learning of age-appropriate skills.	Trying to teach concepts beyond preschooler's understanding.
	Setting stage for creative, spontaneous play.	Demanding rigid, structured play format.
	Encouraging preschooler to try and not to be afraid of mistakes. Encouraging risk taking.	Stressing doing things "right." Discouraging any efforts unless done perfectly.

Points to Remember

1. From birth on, children form beliefs about their self-worth.

2. Treat your child with respect, and expect your child to treat you and others with respect.

3. Encouragement helps children develop self-esteem.

4. Encouragement lets children decide for themselves if they are pleased with what they do. It doesn't demand perfection or make comparisons.

5. Praise and encouragement are *not* the same thing. Praise rewards a child and lets her feel accepted and valued by the parents only when she performs. Encouragement boosts a child and lets her accept and value herself.

6. Be concerned that your children *learn how to learn,* not that they perform perfectly.

7. Don't *push* children. Do encourage them by setting reasonable goals, accepting their efforts, and appreciating their improvements.

8. Show your children that you love them:
   - Tell them so.
   - Show appreciation.
   - Touch them.
   - Spend time with each child—time when you give the child your whole attention.
   - Treat all behavior with respect.

9. Whoever looks after your children needs to have a philosophy similar to yours about caring for them.

10. Parents need to encourage themselves, as well as their children. We all need to value ourselves and face challenges with courage.

Just for You

Your Adult Relationships

Caring for children takes lots of time and energy. As you work to build a respectful, encouraging relationship with your children, don't lose sight of your other relationships. If you're married or in a close relationship, set aside time for that relationship. The amount of time and what you do during it depend on your budget and what child care is available. The two of you could

- talk together after the children are in bed
- take walks
- ride bikes or play a sport together (but leave time to talk)
- have a picnic
- go out to dinner
- get away for a weekend

During your special time together, set aside thoughts of the children. Instead, focus on your relationship. Listen to each other, share feelings, encourage each other, and *have fun together.*

And keep in touch with friends, whether they're other parents of young children, have older children, or have no children. Even occasional phone calls will keep your friendships going.

What will you do this week with your partner? What will you do this week to maintain your friendships?

To learn more about relationships, read Don Dinkmeyer and Jon Carlson, *Time for a Better Marriage* (Circle Pines, Minn.: American Guidance Service, 1984) and *Taking Time for Love* (New York: Prentice Hall, 1989).

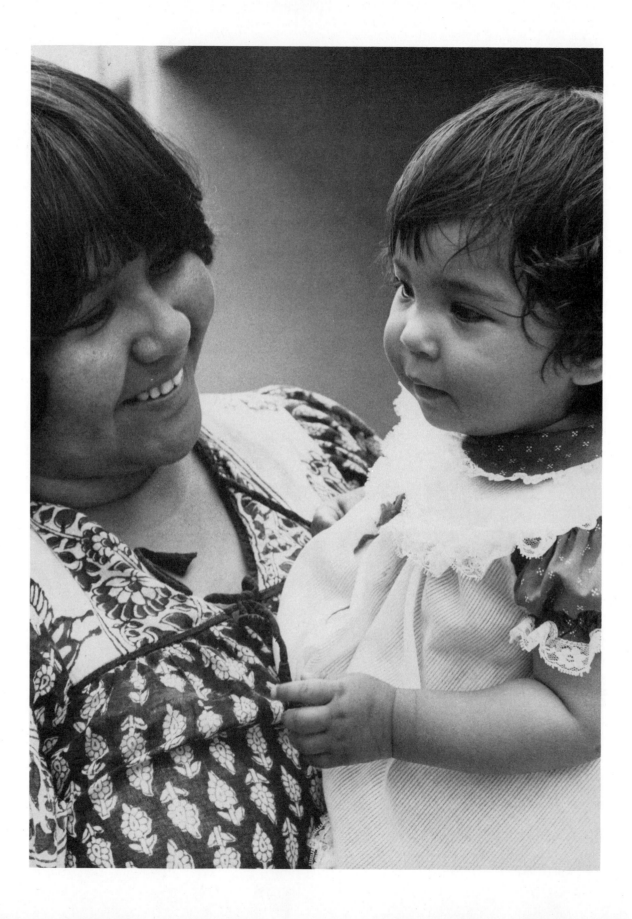

CHAPTER 4

Communicating with Young Children

Throughout *Parenting Young Children* we've stressed the importance of treating children with respect. When we show respect, we let children know they are valued. We give them a model for learning how to deal with other people. And we teach them that their feelings, as well as those of others, are important. In our relations with our children, we want to communicate respect as much and as often as we can.

Consider for a minute these adult situations:

> *Your neighbor, a close friend, comes through your door looking frazzled. "I don't think I can work in that place one more day!" she moans, throwing herself into a chair. By all appearances, your friend is ready to break down. Concerned, you say to her, "You had a bad day. Put up your feet—I'll make us some tea." "I could use some," she tells you gratefully. "You just wouldn't believe what happened this afternoon . . ."*

> *You and your wife and another couple, Jerry and Deb, are watching a game on TV. During an exciting play, Jerry lurches forward in his chair and knocks his soft drink over onto the carpet. Embarrassed, he exclaims, "Oh, no! Look what I did to your rug!" As everyone scurries to get paper towels and clean the mess, you say to your friend, "Don't worry, Jerry—this carpet has seen a lot worse!"*

When friends have problems or make mistakes, we consider their feelings and do what we can to respond helpfully. Even if we feel irritated, or if the time isn't right for us to talk, we make the effort to listen and communicate because we respect them and value their friendship. Do we treat our children the same way?

Talking is one way we communicate. Yet our body language and tone of voice often say more than the words we use. This is especially true with young children. They commonly don't have the words to communicate their feelings and wants. We have to learn to watch their body language—their facial expressions and body movements—to find out what children are trying to get across. Plus, we need to be aware

Imagine if we talked to our friends as we sometimes do to our children.

of what our own body language tells our children. Our actions show children whether or not we understand and respect them.

Listening and speaking are the two halves of the communication process. In this chapter, you will learn how to effectively listen to children and how to express your own feelings respectfully as well.

How to Be an Effective Listener

During our children's lives, we need to do a lot of listening. If we listen well, we can help our children identify, accept, and understand their feelings. We help them discover ways to deal with feelings and problems. And we encourage our children to become effective listeners.

Our role as listener starts when we respond to the first cry after birth. During the following weeks and months, we listen to cries that communicate hunger or tiredness, boredom or fear. We also need to "listen" with our eyes, for babies soon begin to use body language. They may tell us they are happy by smiling. They may tell us they are angry or impatient by twisting away while being dressed. As they grow, babies gradually learn which signals will get them picked up. A toddler knows how to pull an adult to the refrigerator and point out a favorite food. Sometime after their first year, most children begin to speak to us with words. We listen to their first words with wonder and pride. Then later, we hear words come together into full sentences.

Young children ask us to listen for a lot of reasons. Most of their communication is clear and simple, such as "I want a cookie." Our responses are also simple and clear: "Yes, you may" or "No, you may not." Listening is fairly easy when the communication is easily understood.

Sometimes what children want understood may not be clearly stated in their words. A complex message usually has to do with a child's *feelings* about a situation—what the situation means to her. The child wants the meaning heard, understood, and accepted.

This is what we want for ourselves, too. Picture the following situation.

> *Your prized flower garden has been destroyed by a neighbor's pet rabbits. You tell a friend, "My whole garden is ruined! Nothing's left." Your friend says, "Well, what's done is done. Forget it and start over. Anyway, you think you've got problems? You should hear what happened to me yesterday."*

The friend's response shows that he knows your garden is ruined, yet he gives no recognition of your feelings about the situation. He shows no *respect* for your feelings.

You want your feelings to be heard, understood, and accepted. When they are, you believe that your feelings are important and worthy of attention. You receive a message of care and concern. And that invites you to offer care and concern for the feelings of others.

The same is true for your children. They want to be fully heard, too. The way you listen to and express feelings models a skill for your children to develop. Young children find it difficult to see things from someone else's perspective. (Remember, children under five or six are naturally self-centered.) But as they come to know their feelings are valued, they will gradually gain an understanding of others' feelings and of the importance of listening.

Our role as listener starts when we respond to the first cry after birth.

Reflective Listening

To encourage your children to be aware of and trust their own feelings, and to express their feelings constructively, we recommend using *reflective listening.* With reflective listening you *reflect,* like a mirror, the feelings your child is expressing. Reflecting his feelings first helps a child feel he is understood. Later on, it helps him learn the language of feelings and to express his feelings more clearly.

Reflective listening is both an attitude and a skill. As an attitude, it means valuing what your child is feeling and what she has to say. It means being open to the meaning behind your child's words and body language. It means *wanting to understand.*

As a skill, reflective listening is done as follows:

1. Establish eye contact. Let your body position show that you are listening. If your child's eye level is at your knee or your waist, this may mean bending down or picking up the child, or you can both sit down. Stop other tasks, and give the child your whole attention.

2. Hear and define the feeling. After listening with full attention, ask yourself, What is he feeling? Then think of a word that describes that feeling.

3. State the feeling. Now use the feeling word in a sentence. (See "Help Children Find the Words" later in this chapter for some feeling words.) Many people find it easiest to start with a formula for reflective listening:

"You feel ___(state the feeling)___ because ___(state the reason behind the feeling)___ ."

- "You feel sorry because Mikey got hurt."
- "You feel excited because Jane's coming for supper."
- "You feel tired because you worked so hard."
- "You feel happy because the kitty wants to play."

Once you have the "You feel _____ because _____" formula firmly in mind, you may want to use less structured statements:

- "You're sorry that Mikey got hurt."
- "You look excited about Jane coming over."
- "All that hard work really tired you out!"
- "You like playing with Kitty, don't you?"

Reflective listening lets your child know you have heard the feeling and meaning behind the words. Like a mirror, you reflect what you see or hear him saying.

Reflecting feelings in this way lets your child know you have heard the feelings and meaning behind the words. Like a mirror, you reflect what you see or hear him saying.

> *After a delightful morning in the park, your three-year-old daughter stamps her foot and says, "I won't go home!" You are tempted to say, "Oh, yes, you will!" Instead, you use reflective listening and say, "You're disappointed that our playtime is over. You were having so much fun."*

You hear your child's words and see her body language. You use both your knowledge of your child and your common sense to understand the *meaning* of what is said and to reflect it back. Her underlying feelings are recognized, expressed, and accepted.

At times, you won't be sure what your child is feeling. It's okay to make a guess. As long as they sense their parent's sincere interest, children will usually redirect you if you've misinterpreted the feeling.

> *Your son comes home from kindergarten and announces loudly, "School is dumb!" You reply, "Sounds like you're*

angry about something that happened at school today." "I'm not angry," he says with an unhappy frown. "But the teacher doesn't like me." Then he goes on to tell you what was upsetting or difficult.

You use reflective listening to find out the meaning behind his words. If you say instead, "You shouldn't talk that way! School isn't dumb!" he may believe his feelings have been rejected and thus may not feel safe to tell you what happened.

In these examples, children get information about their feelings. Their parents talk about the feelings, so those feelings must be understood. The parents are calm, so the feelings must be normal. Their feelings are not attacked. Feelings are part of normal family conversation. Therefore, it must be okay to have feelings and to show them.

Help Children Find the Words

It's important to begin early to give children a vocabulary of "feeling words." In their first two years, children learn a great deal of language. Along with words for *cup* and *ball,* they need to learn words for their feelings—words like *happy, sad, mad.* As children grow older, they need to learn more specific words for feelings. Knowing the words for her feelings encourages a child's self-understanding and self-acceptance. If she has the words, a child can talk about her feelings. When you reflect a child's feelings by using accurate feeling words, she learns to identify and describe her feelings.

Parents may find it hard to think of words to explain feelings. Here are sample lists of such words.

Words for Reflecting "Upset" Feelings
Note: Using the word *upset* often may communicate that you don't understand. It's best to be more specific.

angry	sad
confused	scared
disappointed	sorry
frightened	unfair
hate	unhappy
hurt	want to get even
left out	want to give up
mad	worried

Words for Reflecting "Happy" Feelings

appreciate	great
better	happy
enjoy	like
excited	love
glad	pleased
good	proud

When to Use Reflective Listening
—And When *Not* To

Reflective listening can be very helpful when a child is feeling strong emotion, either negative or positive, and plainly showing it. A child may use body language (crying, hitting, going rigid, laughing, hugging) or strong words ("I hate you!" "I'm going to run away!" "You're the best dad in the world!").

It's appropriate to use reflective listening when no emotion is apparent, yet you realize the child's feelings are below the surface.

Your four-year-old watches two hours of TV, roams aimlessly around the house, and then demands more TV. You try using reflective listening before responding to her request: "You look like you may be feeling bored. Are you out of ideas for something to do?"

After you've helped her recognize her feeling, she may be better able to come up with other choices for herself.

When you have to deny a child's request, reflective listening is important.[1] Show the child you understand her feelings about the situation, but hold firm to your decision: "I can see that you're angry because I said no TV right now." Don't let the child control you or drag

Our body language and tone of voice often say more than the words we use.

you into an argument: "I know you're mad, but the answer is still no. I'm going to put a load of laundry in now."

Children's feelings need to be understood and respected. However, parents don't need to accept verbal abuse. If your child calls you a name, recognize his anger, but let him know you won't accept insults. "I can hear that you're very angry with me. That's okay—you can say 'I'm angry at you, Mommy.' But I won't listen to you when you call me names." Once you explain your limits, ignore the child if he goes on calling you names. If the behavior continues and ignoring is difficult, you may have to remove the child from the room. You can explain, "I see you've decided not to be around people."

Reflective listening isn't *always* necessary. Remember that most of the time, children's messages are clear and simple. When a child says, "I want a cookie," there is usually no hidden meaning in the words.

It's natural for young children to think they are the center of the world and to expect to be constantly listened to. But this is neither possible nor desirable. Sometimes we are just too busy or too distracted to use reflective listening. It is a challenge to show both that we want to hear what our children have to say and that there are limits to our ability to listen. If you don't have time to listen, say so. Tell the child she can talk to you later: "I can see you're excited and want to tell me more, but I have to make a phone call now. But during supper I'd like to hear all about your trip to the zoo."

Talking So You Are Heard

Reflective listening can help children recognize, accept, and appreciate their feelings. But we also have to effectively communicate our own feelings to them.

Speaking to Children in Encouraging Ways

Chapter 3 talked about encouraging our children. When we have a problem with a child, we need to address the problem in a way that won't discourage the child. We want to share our feelings *without being judgmental.*

> Sid and Marcia are both four years old. Their fathers are
> busy putting up curtain rods in Sid's family's apartment. As

Marcia and Sid run in and out of the living room, the two children grow noisier and noisier. They keep pestering the men for a snack, to tie a shoe, to help locate a lost toy. Finally Sid's father turns to Sid and says, "Quit being such a pest, Sid. How can I ever get this work done?" Marcia's father tells his daughter, "I need to finish helping Sid's daddy here—I can't get you a snack right now. And we can't get the work done when there's noise. I need for you and Sid to play quietly for a while. When we're done working, I'll get you a snack."

Feeling impatient, Sid's father has lashed out at his son. It's understandable that he would do this—we all know how trying it can be to work in the midst of children's noise and demands. But by calling Sid a pest, Sid's father has placed a negative, discouraging label on his son. Further, his irritated reaction, negative as it may be, might actually be serving a goal of attention for Sid.

Marcia's father, on the other hand, has taken a more encouraging, respectful approach. An encouraging parent avoids labels that are judgmental—labels such as "good," "bad," "lazy," "rude," "stubborn," "pest." Marcia's father's response has let his daughter know that he respects her and her needs, but that right now he has to attend to his work. He expects her to cooperate and lets her know of this expectation.

Will Marcia decide to cooperate? If she does, her father may later want to reinforce that positive behavior by saying, "It helped me when you played quietly today while I finished my work." If she doesn't, he can continue to use respectful words and actions to let her know her behavior is not appropriate. In the long run, hearing respectful words will be encouraging for Marcia and will teach her a way of relating to other people.

What kind of respectful words? One very effective way to communicate feelings is with an "I-message."

You-Messages and I-Messages

When talking to our children, we can use "you-messages" or "I-messages."[2] You-messages put down, blame, or nag. They often contain the word *you,* and they attack, insult, or pass judgment on a child: "You should know better." The child who receives lots of you-messages is likely to begin to feel worthless, to fight back, or to stop listening. You-messages tend to discourage cooperation and contribute to lower self-esteem.

I-messages focus on you, rather than your child. They don't label or blame. When you use an I-message, you simply tell how you feel.

A more effective, respectful way of communicating feelings is to use I-messages. I-messages describe how you feel when a child's behavior interferes with your rights. They focus on you, rather than the child. I-messages don't label or blame. When you use an I-message, you simply tell how you feel.

To communicate your feelings in an I-message, follow these three steps:

1. State very specifically what behavior led to your feeling.
2. State what you are feeling.
3. Explain the consequences of the behavior for you.

The Three Parts of an I-Message

Like reflective listening, I-messages have a formula too. When learning to use I-messages, put your words together using these three parts:

1. When   "When I see hitting . . .

2. I feel   I feel worried . . .

3. because   because somebody could get hurt."

- "When toys are left in the driveway, I feel discouraged, because I have to pick them up before I can put the car in the garage."
- "When I hear so much crying, I feel confused, because I can't understand what you're trying to say to me."

I-messages help children focus on how their actions are being received. Communicating your feelings in a respectful manner encourages your children to be respectful of others' feelings and rights. By using I-messages, you show the importance of sharing feelings in a constructive way.

I-messages like these are most appropriate when used with older toddlers and with preschoolers. To form understandable I-messages for younger children, you may want to simplify what you say:
- "I don't like having my nose pulled. It hurts."
- "I get a headache listening to so much noise."

Here are some more examples of I-messages.

Two-year-old Carmen runs into the street. After carrying her back to the sidewalk, her father reacts by saying, "I get scared when you run into the street. A car could hit you and you would get hurt."

With this I-message, Carmen is given information about what she did, how her father feels, and why he feels that way. At two, Carmen is too young to really understand how her dad feels. But she hears and can sense the emotion behind his tone of voice when he talks about feeling scared. She may also begin to connect running into the street with her father's fear. In this way she will gradually be increasing her knowledge of the feeling of fear.

And Dad's I-message is also an effective model for teaching respect for the feelings of others. Parental feelings need to be communicated in I-messages throughout childhood. When messages are delivered to them respectfully, children are more likely over time to develop an attitude of respect for others. They also learn to communicate their own feelings respectfully.

Pedro refuses to share his toys with Zach, another four-year-old. His mother responds with an I-message. "Pedro, when you won't let Zach play with any toys, I feel annoyed, because the fighting keeps interrupting my work. And it looks like Zach feels hurt that you won't share any toys with him."

This I-message may or may not solve the problem. From it, Pedro receives information about how his behavior affects two different people. Because he is being talked to respectfully, Pedro's self-respect isn't damaged, and he is better able to focus on problem solving.

Avoid Angry I-Messages
It's important to keep hostile feelings out of your I-messages. If you send angry messages, it's very hard for children to feel they *aren't* being blamed for your anger. Often anger is the result of other feelings not being expressed. You may start out feeling disappointed, for example, but not say anything. Then you dwell on it and make yourself angry. You can avoid hostile messages by expressing the feelings linked to your anger.

You are in the store with your three-year-old, and she wanders off. You're afraid something has happened to her. But by the time you find her, you have worked yourself into a rage. Instead of acting on your anger, you choose to express your fear. You give her a hug and say, "Oh, thank goodness you're safe! I was really scared something had happened to you! Please stay close to Daddy."

> *Children need safety guidelines stated, restated, and reinforced over many years.*

In dangerous situations like this, don't assume that your child has learned her lesson about safety. Children need safety guidelines stated, restated, and reinforced over many years. Remember, young children won't necessarily understand the problem from your point of view. Nevertheless, using I-messages helps them feel respected. It shows that while you are upset by unacceptable behavior, you value and appreciate your child enough to deal with the problem without yelling, blaming, or threatening. A child who consistently hears I-messages as a means of addressing problems is more likely, as she grows older, to appreciate the needs and feelings of others.

Send Friendly I-Messages Too!

I-messages are also appropriate in communicating positive feelings, not just negative ones.

Suppose your three-year-old spills juice and cleans it up himself. You can say to him, "I'm happy when you clean up your spilled juice. It shows you can do it yourself."

Again, the child is getting feedback on how his behavior is being received. (He is also getting positive attention and encouragement!)

Here are some other examples of friendly I-messages:
- "It sure feels good to come home to your happy smile today."
- "I noticed when you let Sissy hold your doll. It's nice you're learning to share."

Keep Your Expectations Realistic

It's very important to keep in mind that young children won't necessarily understand everything you are saying in your I-message. The younger your child, the simpler the message needs to be.

Both reflective listening and I-messages are ways of communicating. They are not ways to get what we want from our children. They are ways to guide, not to control. Our children may or may not stop unpleasant behavior because they've been understood or because they understand us.

Reflective listening and I-messages improve communication. They can influence behavior in a particular situation. They don't guarantee better behavior.

When to Begin Using Reflective Listening and I-Messages

We believe it makes sense to use these methods of communication with even the youngest infants. Very young children will miss the meaning of the words. But they will not miss the supportive attitude shown in parents' voices and faces.

- "I see you like your bath."
- "Oh, you reached for the rattle!"
- "When you pull the kitty's tail, it hurts her."
- "If you open your mouth, the food will go in easier. And you won't feel so mad and hungry."

Starting early also gives us practice so that when our children begin to talk, we are already comfortable with listening and speaking in this style. Using reflective listening and I-messages will help establish an atmosphere of mutual respect between you and your baby or toddler. These methods will also help your preschooler grow less self-centered and begin to understand and respect the feelings of others.

Notes

1. Stanley Greenspan and Nancy Thorndike Greenspan, *First Feelings* (New York: Viking Penguin, 1985), p. 211.

2. Thomas Gordon, *Parent Effectiveness Training* (New York: Peter H. Wyden, 1970), pp. 115-16.

Activity for the Week

Use reflective listening and I-messages regularly and observe the results.

Be sure to reflect and express positive feelings, too.

Chart 4

Reflective Listening and I-Messages

Use reflective listening and I-messages to help children feel respected. Over time, communicating in these ways can help them understand what they feel and how you feel.

	Reflective Listening	I-Messages
Babies		
Use feeling vocabulary with infants. Respond to their nonverbal messages, and let them begin to learn how they are feeling. Though babies won't understand many of your words, they will sense your feelings.	"You can't reach the ball—you feel angry." "You're scared the doggy will bite." "You're very happy to have your bear."	"When you feel sick, I feel sad." "When I see you smiling, I feel happy, too!" "I wish I knew why you're crying."
Toddlers		
Since toddlers are becoming verbal, respond more to their words. Yet still watch their behavior to pick up their feelings.	"You sound pretty angry with me because I said no cookies." "You're really excited to get to play with Jimmy." "Your face says you're sad—do you think this is unfair?"	"When I don't know why you're crying, I don't know how to help." "When you say you don't love me, I feel sad, but I still love you." "When you throw toys, I worry that something might get broken."
Preschoolers		
Preschoolers' ability to reason is better developed. Respond more to verbal messages but still look for nonverbal ones. Use more specific responses to their feelings than the general *mad, upset, angry, sad,* and *glad.* You can guess how preschoolers feel—they will usually redirect you if you're wrong.	"You look disappointed about not winning the game. Want to talk about it?" "Is it possible that you're feeling left out?" "It's nice to feel like the teacher appreciated your help during circle time."	"I feel good when you put your toys away. It shows that you want to help." "Your running on the wet sidewalk scares me. It's slippery, and you might fall and get hurt." "When you play nicely with your friends, I feel happy, because you are showing me that you can get along with others."

Points to Remember

1. We all communicate with words and body language. Young children use body language long before they can speak.

2. Sometimes children want to communicate their feelings about a situation but don't have the words to do it.

3. We can use reflective listening to learn the underlying meaning in a child's words. Like a mirror, we reflect what the child says.

4. Follow this formula to learn to use reflective listening: *"You feel* ___state the feeling___ *because* ___(state the reason behind the feeling)___ *."*
   - "You feel sorry because Mikey got hurt."
   - "You feel excited because Jane's coming for supper."

5. Children need to hear and learn words for their feelings.

6. Reflective listening is helpful when a child expresses emotions or when you believe the child has feelings that are not being expressed.

7. Avoid using you-messages, which blame or put down a child. Instead, use I-messages, which tell how you feel and don't blame anyone.

8. Follow this formula to learn to use I-messages:

   When   "When I see hitting . . .

   I feel   I feel worried . . .

   because   because somebody could get hurt."

9. Reflective listening and I-messages are ways to communicate with and influence your children. They are not methods of control or guarantees of better behavior.

Just for You

Straight Talk in Adult Relationships

Many of us expect our spouses or close friends to read our minds—to know what we're feeling or what we want without our telling them. But they can't! Effective communication between adults calls for straight talk. That means communicating accurately what we feel and want, without blaming the other person or demanding that he or she follow our wishes. I-messages are a form of straight talk, and may be used with adults as well as with children.

When we share our feelings about how someone else's behavior affects us, we are being honest and communicating mutual respect. Suppose your partner always puts dirty dishes in the sink without scraping them—on your night to wash dishes. This creates extra work for you. You could say, "When I find unscraped dishes in the sink, I really get discouraged, because it takes me extra time and effort to get them clean." You haven't blamed your partner—you've simply shared your feelings.

If your partner doesn't respond, you could make a clear statement about what you want: "I'd prefer the dishes be scraped so I can get the job done quickly." If the problem still isn't solved, it's time to negotiate—a skill you'll practice in Chapter 5's "Just for You."

Simply put, straight talk
- tells directly what you want ("I want a hug." "I would like some time to talk.")
- states your intention ("I'll wash what I find in the hamper." "I'll cook supper if you'll make the salad.")
- is friendly in intent and tone of voice—even when it is firm

Think of recent situations in your adult relationships in which you've been silent when you needed to speak. Think of times when you've spoken, but in blameful ways.

Begin this week to practice straight talk. But don't overdo it—take it one step at a time.

To learn more about maintaining your adult relationships, read Don Dinkmeyer and Jon Carlson, *Time for a Better Marriage* (Circle Pines, Minn.: American Guidance Service, 1984) and *Taking Time for Love* (New York: Prentice Hall, 1989).

CHAPTER 5

Helping Young Children Learn to Cooperate

Our children are growing up to be part of a larger world. We want them to feel good about themselves, to be able to communicate easily and effectively, and to find a satisfying place within that world. None of these things, however, can happen independently of the others. To live comfortably and contribute in a family, in a community, and beyond, all people need to learn to cooperate with each other.

Like most life skills, cooperative attitudes and behavior develop gradually, over time. With our help, children can begin to understand what it means to cooperate. They can see and start to learn ways to cooperate with parents, siblings, and other children. One of our jobs as parents is to model cooperative behavior and nurture its growth in our children.

What Is Cooperation?

Parents often use the word "cooperate" when what they actually mean is "obey."

> *Three-and-a-half-year-old Jenna is fooling around at the dinner table. She is busy singing, feeding the cat, grabbing her sister's toast, and just generally doing everything but eating and sharing in conversation with the rest of her family. Her father has told Jenna several times to turn around, leave her sister and the cat alone, eat her dinner. Finally fed up, Dad yells at his daughter, "I want you to cooperate, young lady! Sit still and eat—or else! And not another word out of you!"*

Parents often use the word "cooperate" when what they actually mean is "obey."

Although Dad has said he wants cooperation, it's obvious that what he really wants is for Jenna to mind. Yelling and threatening may bring this about—for a while. But Jenna's father could teach his daughter something much more useful by encouraging Jenna to *cooperate* with others at the table.

Cooperation means working together to meet the needs of a situation. It does *not* mean that children do what adults command. There are many ways to help our children learn cooperative attitudes and

If we understand the needs and limitations that are part of being a child, then we can set realistic expectations for our children and ourselves.

behavior. We want to use methods that both encourage positive behavior and discourage negative behavior. This chapter looks at ways parents can teach and encourage children to cooperate in solving the problems of living together.

How Much Cooperation Can Parents Expect?

We've already noted that cooperation is something that grows gradually. To nurture this growth, it's good to know something about children's development and how this relates to their ability to cooperate. If we understand the needs and limitations that are part of being a child, then we can set realistic expectations for our children and ourselves.

Effective approaches by parents help children learn self-control. This internal control shows itself in a sense of responsibility and a spirit of cooperation. Let's consider what kind of cooperation we can expect from babies, toddlers, and preschoolers, and what kinds of methods will be effective in helping them develop cooperative behavior.

Babies

Babies are explorers. Every setting is new territory to explore. Babies use all their senses—sight, hearing, smell, touch, taste—to take in a situation. They are explorers without rules or common sense. In part, they explore to find boundaries.

Babies are explorers . . . without rules or common sense. In part, they explore to find boundaries.

Babies see themselves as the center of the universe. They have no understanding of the needs and rights of others. Because of this, babies can't be expected to *naturally* cooperate. But babyhood is the perfect time to begin teaching cooperation. During your baby's first year, every interaction you have with him is a chance to show mutual respect and encourage cooperation.

> *Mom is giving a bath to eight-month-old Pablo. She says, "You like it when I wash your arm with the soft cloth. Now you wash my arm. I like it too!" And she guides the baby's hand to wash her arm.*

> *After five-month-old Tricia is fed, her dad puts her in the infant seat. He says, "I fed you—now you're fine. But I'm hungry! You can help me. Keep me company and play while I eat."*

Pablo and Tricia won't necessarily understand and cooperate. Pablo may prefer to pull on his mother's earrings. Tricia may squawk and fuss, making Dad's meal less than pleasant and herself less than companionable! As we teach the beginnings of cooperation, we deal with the beginnings of effective discipline. Babies are very determined, but they never intend to manipulate. Their behavior simply reflects their attempts to communicate their needs. Because of this, we do not consider their behavior negative, just naturally immature. Babies need adults to set and uphold boundaries that will keep them physically and psychologically safe. Setting boundaries is the most loving and effective form of discipline for babies.

Even as they set limits, parents can stress cooperation.

> *If Pablo pulls at his mother's earrings, she can remove them and tell her son, "I know you don't want to hurt me—and I don't want you to! Are you ready to wash my arm now?" If he's not ready, Mother can respect that and simply continue with his bath. In these ways she models cooperation even as she keeps necessary limits in place.*

Babies can be very determined.

Toddlers need protective boundaries, maybe even more so than babies. They can move faster and farther than babies, but they don't have self-control or recognize dangers.

Toddlers

Toddlers still like to explore. But they become aware of a cause and effect in their actions: "When I run, you chase me. When I scream, you cringe. When I cry, you hug." Toddlers start being able to predict the consequences of their behavior. Then they start being able to change their behavior in order to change the consequences. Most toddlers know how to get a rise out of their parents. Whether they're eating dog food or tearing pages out of books, the look in their eye tells you when their actions are directed at *you*.

Toddlers need protective boundaries, maybe even more so than babies. They can move faster and farther than babies, but they don't have self-control and they don't recognize dangers. Although they continue to need clear physical boundaries, toddlers also need to be learning social boundaries. They can begin to understand messages about what is and is not acceptable behavior.

Toddlers have a very simple sense of what it means to cooperate. They also frequently act in ways that appear totally uncooperative. Early on, the toddler may show signs of beginning to assert herself and become independent. The toddler's self-assertion helps her develop self-esteem. With the start of self-assertion may come the first signs of what is called *negativism*. The toddler may refuse to do what is asked, or may do the opposite of what is asked. The toddler is learning that she has control over herself. She may show this by closing her mouth firmly when a parent wants her to open it for her last bite of food. She may run away when she is asked to come put her shirt on. She is learning to say "No!"—loudly, and often. The toddler is not being defiantly hostile. She's just learning what she can and can't do as she moves toward independence.

Psychologist Fitzhugh Dodson describes negativism as a passing phase between babyhood and early childhood. Handled appropriately, it can be a positive phase in a child's development. Without it, a child would remain stuck in babyhood. You can deal with negativism by helping redirect a child to positive activities that build independence and self-esteem.[1] These are activities at which he can succeed and for which he can be recognized. In doing this, you can also build cooperation.

> *Grandfather finds two-and-a-half-year-old Matt being rough with the family pet. He says, "I see you're petting the dog. She likes to be petted, doesn't she? Would you like to help me brush her? That's right—gentle, not hard. Like this."*

———

Kim, a very active two-year-old, is being loud and wild. Her mother picks Kim up and holds her. She tells the toddler, "Running and shouting are fine in the park, but not in the apartment. I need to wash dishes now. You can help me. Then we'll go to the park."

Preschoolers

Preschoolers are better able than toddlers to predict the consequences of their behavior and to use some degree of self-control. While toddlers usually need physical action by parents that limits their behavior, preschoolers begin to be influenced by words alone. Passion rules toddlers. Reason plays a part in preschoolers' behavior. Toddlers often act or react, and put up with the consequences. Preschoolers have some ability to change their behavior to avoid unwanted consequences.

Because preschoolers can be more rational, they can be given expectations. They can be given clear, simple rules and the conse-

It's not reasonable to expect completely cooperative behavior from preschoolers, but the seeds of cooperative behavior that were planted in babyhood are beginning to sprout.

quences of breaking them. They won't understand your expectations every time or in every situation, but their understanding is growing.

During the preschool years, our children may begin to notice our attempts to teach cooperation. It's not reasonable to expect completely cooperative preschoolers. We can expect the *beginnings* of cooperative behavior. It is natural for preschoolers to still believe their needs and wishes come first. But the seeds of cooperative behavior that were planted in babyhood are beginning to sprout.

Who Owns the Problem?

Wherever there are parents and children, there are problems. When problems arise concerning a child's behavior, parents can ask themselves, Who does this problem belong to? Me? Or my child? In other words, who "owns" the problem?

The person who owns a problem is responsible for handling it.[2] Parents of young children often feel they own all their children's problems. But when parents try to solve all problems, they deny their children the chance to learn how to be responsible for themselves. It's also impossible for any parent to be "Super Problem Solver." Recognizing who owns a problem helps you decide what, if any, action to take.

How do parents determine which problems belong to them and which to their children?

To decide who owns a problem, ask yourself four questions:
1. Does the problem interfere with my rights as a person?
2. Does it involve the safety of my child or others?
3. Does it involve the protection of property?
4. Is my child developmentally incapable of "owning" or solving the problem?

If the answer to any *one* of these questions is *yes,* then you own the problem. If the answer to *each* of the questions is *no,* then your child may own the problem—depending on her age.

In the case of babies and young toddlers, parents will often find that they, the parents, own most of the problems. But ownership of many problems can be transferred as children grow older.

> *If your nine-month-old has a wet diaper, it's your problem: it involves your child's safety (health). But if your five-year-old*

wets his pants, it's his problem (assuming he has no diagnosed physical difficulty with bladder control). He needs to change and clean himself to learn to be responsible for himself.

———

If your one-year-old is crying because she's hungry, it's your problem. But if your four-year-old won't eat her lunch, then an hour later complains she's hungry, it's her problem.

Examples of Parent-Owned Problems

Four-year-old Gretchen is making the morning more and more difficult. She refuses to dress herself and dawdles over her cereal. Gretchen's mother can barely get her to the sitter and then get to work without being late.

———

Dad walks into the baby's room to get the baby up from his nap. He finds three-year-old Amy poking hard at the baby and pulling the baby's hair.

———

Two-year-old Ben's parents discover that he has colored on the wall in the kitchen.

Examples of Child-Owned Problems

Two-year-old Peter wants to play with Whiskers, the family cat. But whenever Peter comes near, Whiskers takes off like a flash—and Peter bursts into tears!

———

Five-year-old Erin wanders sadly into the living room, where her stepfather is studying. "There's nothin' to do," she tells him grumpily. "Will you play with me?"

———

Mom hears a wail from the bedroom. She hurries in and finds her three-year-old daughter, Ginny, surrounded by toys and crying her heart out. A little apart from Ginny sits her friend Isaac, who is busily playing with Ginny's favorite stuffed rabbit. "Rabbie," cries Ginny to her mother. "I want my Rabbie!"

What About Babies?

The younger our children are, the more they depend on us for their care. Meeting their needs is our problem because there is so little they can do for themselves. Yet, what they can do, they need to be allowed to do. If it is beyond a baby's skill to do something, then she needs and deserves help. If she can do something on her own, let her build her budding sense of belief in self.

Six-month-old Susie wants the rattle that lies just beyond her grasp. She struggles to reach it. Susie's mother sees her daughter stretching for the rattle, but she doesn't pick it up and give it to the infant. Instead, she encourages Susie's efforts to get the rattle herself. In this way, she lets Susie own the problem of getting her rattle.

When three-month-old Gregor cries because he's hungry, his dad feeds him. Later, Gregor fusses slightly in his crib at naptime. His dad doesn't go to the baby immediately but allows Gregor a few minutes to comfort himself.

Sometimes parents may want to let the child cope on his own. At other times, parents will want to help the child find a solution.

Cooperating to Solve Problems

Deciding who owns problems gives parents reasonable expectations for themselves. It gives children a healthy separateness. Deciding problem ownership is also a tool that helps parents know what to do next. When parents own the problem, they need to take action. In the case of child-owned problems, it will depend. Sometimes parents may want to let the child cope on his own. At other times, parents will want to help the child find a solution.

When you or your child owns a problem, you may do one or more of the following:
- Ignore the problem.
- Use reflective listening or an I-message.
- Make sure your child knows the consequence of her behavior.
- Explore alternatives with the child.

Exploring Alternatives

In the last chapter, we discussed how reflective listening and I-messages can help solve or lessen behavior problems. But they may not always be enough. Parents can also use a method called *exploring alternatives.* Exploring alternatives doesn't mean that parents solve all the problems. It is, however, one method of looking at—and helping children look at—different ways to solve a problem.

No matter who owns a problem, there are five basic steps that can be helpful in finding a solution to it:[3]

1. Understand the problem. Make sure it is clear to both you and your child. Use reflective listening or I-messages to make clear your feelings and your child's feelings.

2. Use brainstorming to find possible solutions (alternatives). Suggest ways to solve the problem. Ask your child for suggestions, or guide him by offering tentative suggestions ("What might happen if you . . . ?").

3. Consider the suggested solutions. What do you think of each possible solution? What does your child think of each one?

4. Choose a solution. You and your child (if she's old enough) decide together which solution you can both accept.

5. Make or obtain a commitment to a solution and set a time to evaluate it. You and your child both commit yourselves to accept a solution. Decide together how long to use the solution. Set a specific time to talk about how it's working.

With very young children, you will want to explore alternatives as simply and briefly as possible. For example, in brainstorming, you may guide your child to find only two or three possible solutions. You may even accept a single suggestion, if it seems workable.

> *Three-year-old Caitlin has been playing with her dolls in the kitchen. As her mom and dad start to fix dinner, the dolls are in the way. Caitlin's parents tell her, "We can't fix supper with all your babies in here. What shall we do?" "But they're sleeping," cries Caitlin. "It's naptime." "I think they might sleep better somewhere quieter," suggests Dad. "I know where," says Caitlin. She busily begins to transfer the dolls to a favorite spot behind the couch in the living room, and Mom and Dad get on with supper.*

Often, too, situations can be handled by giving the child a simple choice: "If you want to play at Joyce's, you need to pick up your toys

With very young children, you will want to explore alternatives as simply and briefly as possible.

first." "Can you two solve this problem fairly, or do you need to stop playing now?"

Let's look at examples of ways to deal with parent-owned and child-owned problems.

Dealing with Problems the Parent Owns

The goal of problem solving is to find an effective solution that's respectful to both you and your child. Children are more likely to cooperate when they feel that they have some power and choice in a situation and that their feelings and wishes are valued. Which action you choose depends on the child's age, the type of problem, and how frequently the problem happens.

> *When you pick up sixteen-month-old Nicholas, he knocks your glasses off. You put them back on carefully and say, "When my glasses are knocked off, I'm afraid they'll break." A few minutes later, Nicholas knocks the glasses off again. You gently place Nicholas on the floor and tell him, "I can't let you grab my glasses, so I'm putting you down." Later, when Nicholas wants to be picked up again, you can give him another chance. "Do you want to sit on my lap again? Okay. But if you grab my glasses, I will put you down."*

Here, you used an I-message, stated consequences, and followed through. Nicholas hasn't had much practice at controlling his behavior, so he will probably grab the glasses again. Knowing what will happen helps him learn control. Whenever Nicholas grabs, he gets put down. He begins to learn why. He chooses the consequence of his action.

> *Four-year-old Sofia interrupts her mother's phone conversation. Her mother says, "When I'm interrupted, I feel confused. It's hard to talk to more than one person at a time. What could you do instead if you want my attention?" She and Sofia come up with three alternatives:*
> *1. Before making a call, her mother can check with Sofia to see if she thinks she will need something during the phone conversation.*
> *2. Sofia can wait patiently for an agreed upon time until the call is over. Then her mother can listen just to her.*
> *3. If Sofia has to communicate, she can draw a picture of what she wants.*

Here, Mother began exploring alternatives with her daughter. A four-year-old may have lots of suggestions if she truly feels her ideas are being asked for and if she doesn't feel put down. After choosing and using an alternative, the problem may still continue. Then a different action will be needed. Mother and Sofia will have to explore alternatives further. They'll need to come to an understanding about a specific consequence if Sofia continues her misbehavior.

Five-year-old Luis won't accept his eight o'clock bedtime. His dad thinks Luis is old enough to negotiate a more formal solution to the problem. He uses the five steps for exploring alternatives.

Step 1 *(Understanding problem)*
Dad: *Luis, bedtime has gotten to be quite a problem around here. When you keep coming out of your room, your mom and I feel upset because we don't get to have our time alone together. How do you feel?*
Luis: *I don't like to be alone. I want to be with you guys.*
Dad: *So you feel lonesome. You like it better being here with us, huh?*

Step 2 *(Brainstorming possible alternatives)*
Let's think of some ways we can solve this problem. (Possibilities include spending more time with Luis before his bedtime, letting him stay up later one night a week, letting him stay up as late as he wants, letting him listen to a tape to keep him company while he goes to sleep.)

Step 3 *(Considering suggested solutions)*
Dad: *Let's look at the list and see which ideas we both think are fair.*

Step 4 *(Choosing solution)*
Luis: *I wanna stay up.*
Dad: *But I worry that you won't get the sleep you need. What else might work instead?*
Luis: *Can I play a story?*
Dad: *On the tape player?*
Luis: *Uh-huh.*
Dad: *Okay—I'm willing to try that. Let's write an agreement to show we are both willing to work together.*

Step 5 *(Setting commitment and evaluation)*
Sample Agreement
1. Luis will go to his bedroom at eight o'clock, his bedtime. He will play a story on the tape player and listen in bed with the lights off. He will leave his room only to use the bathroom.
2. Before Luis's bedtime, Mom and Dad will spend fifteen minutes with him, reading stories and playing games. If Luis leaves his room after eight o'clock, he will be choosing not to have that special time together the next evening.

_____   _____

(parent's signature)   *(child's mark)*

Dad: *Shall we use our agreement for three nights? Then we can talk about how it's working out.*

If the problem hasn't improved after three nights, Dad and Luis can use a different solution. Mom and Dad may need to take turns spending more time with Luis at night—especially if they don't have other opportunities during the day to be with their son. Additional reflective listening may reveal that Luis is afraid of something in his room. Luis and his parents may need to explore alternatives again. Over time, though, cooperation in exploring alternatives and testing solutions will probably help this family solve the problem. Children who are old enough to write their names often like the idea of a written agreement. If not, just agree verbally on what you will do.

Our goal is to increase our children's sense of responsibility for solving their own problems.

Dealing with Problems the Child Owns

Our goal is to increase our children's sense of responsibility for solving their own problems. Let's look at some examples of problems owned by children at various ages.

> *Eighteen-month-old Mariko can't reach her bear on top of the dresser. Her father says, "What would happen if you pulled your stool over to the dresser and stood on it? Would you be tall enough then?" After she moves the stool and gets the bear, Father says, "Look what you learned, Mariko! You learned how to get your bear off the dresser."*

We want our children to begin learning to count on themselves to solve some of their problems. Find ways to encourage children. Focus on their learning new skills and behavior.

Two-and-a-half-year-old Carl doesn't want his parents to go out for the evening. They notice his feelings and offer to read to him for a few minutes before they leave. Carl isn't satisfied with that and throws a tantrum. He screams and hits his parents. His parents say, "You're really angry that we're going out. We'd like to look at a book with you first. But we can't read a story unless you stop screaming, Carl. If you don't stop, we won't have time to read to you."

Carl's parents reflect their son's feelings—he knows he's been heard. The consequences of his actions are explained to Carl. Then it becomes his choice which action to take. Even with these encouraging actions, Carl's parents may not succeed in stopping the tantrum. But the respect and willingness to cooperate they have shown will be more helpful in the long run than either giving in or yelling back.

When a lion at the zoo roars loudly, three-year-old Nina hides behind her mother. Her mother says, "It's very scary when a lion roars like that. What would help you feel less scared?" Nina suggests they hold hands tightly. After they try it and Nina relaxes a little, her mother says, "Your idea worked. You look happier now."

The playmates of four-year-old Elvin have told him to go home. His dad gives Elvin time to tell the story of what happened and to talk about his feelings. Then Elvin and his dad discuss what to do about the problem. Elvin suggests, "I could blow up their houses! Or I could stay inside by myself all day." His dad helps him consider the consequences of such alternatives. "If you blow up their houses, then what will happen? If you stay inside all day, what will you do?"

The more Elvin is guided to think about the results of his possible actions, the more skilled he will become at picking satisfactory alternatives.

Hold Family Discussions

One of the most effective ways to teach and practice cooperation at home is by holding regular family meetings. Though formal family meetings aren't practical with very young children, parents can help them become used to the idea through brief, structured *family discussions*. The discussions might be used to help in solving problems. But they are not meant to be used *only* for solving problems. Parents and young children can use brief family discussions to

- plan family fun
- distribute chores
- make decisions about family issues
- give encouragement
- express feelings and concerns

How much a child takes part in family discussions depends on her age and maturity.

Babies can take part simply by being present during discussions. As they grow, they will get used to the meetings and be able to participate more.

Toddlers and preschoolers can handle discussions that are brief and take place often. They can concentrate if discussion centers on one issue and a simple decision is to be made. Because young children have short memories, it's best if any decision made at the meeting is put into practice right after the meeting. If that's not possible, a reminder about the decision can be given to children later.

Parents and children may discuss when the children are to take their baths—before supper or just before bedtime. The family may decide that the children will bathe before bedtime. If the discussion has been held a few hours before bedtime, the parents may need to remind the children of the decision just before it's time to bathe.

With preschoolers or slightly older children, parents may want to begin to introduce a more formal structure. It's still important to keep the discussion short and simple. Use this basic format:

- Start on a positive note. Share what's new and good in each person's life, or tell what you appreciate about one another.

    Mom thanks four-year-old Jesse for a gift he made her in school. Jesse says he can't wait for his birthday to come. Dad points out what fun the baby is having playing with toy shapes on the floor. Six-year-old Heather says, "And I got to feed her today! Boy was that messy!"

- Discuss "old business." The family can agree that bedtime baths seem to be working, or decide to change bathtime for one or both of the children.
- Discuss "new business." This family might discuss plans for Jesse's upcoming birthday party.

Any agreements or decisions made in a family discussion are binding until the next meeting. It's important that the meetings or discussions take place regularly so children can learn to keep agreements over a period of time.*

Take the Long View

Always keep in mind that our children are developing skills and understanding *gradually*. So are we! Working to cooperate with those around us is a lifelong process. Through our example and practice, we can create an environment for our children that will nurture the growth of respect and cooperation.

---

*For more information on family meetings and meetings with older children, see Don Dinkmeyer and Gary D. McKay, *Systematic Training for Effective Parenting (STEP): The Parent's Handbook,* 3rd ed. (Circle Pines, Minn.: American Guidance Service, 1989), pp. 103-13.

Notes

1. Fitzhugh Dodson, *How to Parent* (New York: New American Library, 1973).

2. Thomas Gordon, *Parent Effectiveness Training* (New York: Peter H. Wyden, 1970), p. 63.

3. Don Dinkmeyer et al., *The Effective Parent* (Circle Pines, Minn.: American Guidance Service, 1987), pp. 113-14.

Activity for the Week

Identify who owns any problems that occur. Explore alternatives where appropriate.

Chart 5

Who Owns the Problem?

To determine problem ownership, ask yourself: "Does this problem interfere with my rights as a person? Does it involve the safety of my child or others? Does it involve the protection of property? Is my child developmentally incapable of 'owning' or solving the problem?" If the answer to any *one* of these questions is *yes,* then you own the problem. If the answer to *each* of the questions is *no,* then your child may own the problem—depending on her age.

	Situation	Who Owns Problem?	Appropriate Parental Response
Infants	The younger the child, the more likely it is that the parent will own the problem. With an infant, more safety and developmental concerns take precedence. If your six-month-old is crying because he is hungry or wet, you own the problem because it involves the safety (health) of your child.		
Toddlers	Fourteen-month-old wants a cookie but Daddy doesn't want him to have one, so toddler throws a tantrum.	Child	First, use reflective listening: "I see you are really angry that you're not getting a cookie." Then, explore alternatives: "You may have a banana or an apple." Third, ignore the tantrum if child persists.
	Toddler refuses to be buckled into car seat.	Parent	Child must be buckled in for safety: "You don't like the car seat, but to be safe, you must be buckled in."
	Toddler chooses to wear shorts on cold day.	Child	Toddler will go outside and come back in when cold: "I see you got cold. Would you like to put some long pants on so you won't be as cold when you go back outside?"
Preschoolers	Two three-year-olds fight over toy.	Child	"I see you both want to play with the toy. Can you think of a way to share it?" If they don't cooperate, separate them or send one child home. If there is no hitting, let them work it out on their own.
	Four-year-old spills his juice.	Child	Give him the opportunity to clean up spill.
	Five-year-old refuses to take prescribed medication or go to doctor.	Parent	Child needs to take medication or go to doctor. "It is very important that you take this medication and that we see Dr. Day. Then you will feel better."

Points to Remember

1. Cooperation means working together to meet the needs of a situation.

2. From the time they are babies, we can help our children learn cooperative attitudes and behavior.

3. Children develop skills of cooperation and problem solving gradually, over time.

4. Babies need physical boundaries. They can't naturally cooperate, but they can begin to learn about cooperation.

5. Toddlers need physical and social boundaries. They begin to assert themselves and may exhibit negativism—refusing to do what is asked or doing the opposite of what is asked.

6. Preschoolers have some degree of self-control. They can understand the consequences of their behavior and have some ability to change their behavior to avoid the consequences.

7. The person who owns a problem is responsible for handling it. Sometimes that's the parent, sometimes the child.

8. To decide who owns a problem, ask yourself four questions:
   - Does the problem interfere with my rights as a person?
   - Does it involve the safety of my child or others?
   - Does it involve the protection of property?
   - Is my child developmentally incapable of "owning" or solving the problem?

   Any one "yes" answer means a parent-owned problem.
   Four "no" answers mean a child-owned problem.

9. Whether you or your child owns a problem, there are various possible actions you can take to find a solution:
   - Ignore the problem.
   - Use reflective listening or an I-message.
   - Make sure your child knows the consequence of her behavior.
   - Explore alternatives with the child.

10. Exploring alternatives is a method of looking at solutions to a problem. It has five steps:
    - Understand the problem.
    - Use brainstorming to find possible solutions (alternatives).
    - Consider the suggested solutions.
    - Choose a solution.
    - Make or obtain a commitment to a solution and set a time to evaluate.

11. We want to help our children develop a sense of responsibility for solving their own problems.

12. The family meeting can create a feeling of unity and help with problem solving. With your young child, use brief family discussions.

Handling Conflict in Adult Relationships

Exploring alternatives can be used to address problems with children. It can also be used when a conflict occurs with a spouse, a friend, or a relative. You can use the steps for exploring alternatives to negotiate agreements:*

1. Understand the problem.

2. Use brainstorming to find possible solutions (alternatives).

3. Consider the suggested solutions.

4. Choose a solution.

5. Make or obtain a commitment to a solution and set a time to evaluate.

Rudolf Dreikurs, a psychiatrist and author, identified four important principles for handling conflict:**

1. Maintain mutual respect. Avoid fighting or giving in. Use reflective listening and I-messages.

2. Identify the real issue. You may be discussing money or sharing responsibilities. But what's being discussed is seldom the *real issue*. Many times the real issue is who's right, who'll be in charge, or fairness. You can say something like, "It seems to me we're both interested in being right. I wonder how this will help us solve the problem."

3. Change the agreement. In a conflict, the persons involved have made an agreement to quarrel. You can change the agreement by *changing your own behavior*. Be willing to compromise if necessary.

4. Invite participation in decision making. An agreement comes when both persons suggest solutions and settle on one both are willing to accept. If this doesn't happen, all you can do is state your intentions: "Since we aren't willing to find a solution acceptable to both of us, then I choose to ___(state your intention)___." Your intentions simply tell what *you* will do—not what the other person is to do.

If you have a conflict in your adult relationships you'd like to resolve, decide how to use the steps for exploring alternatives and the principles of conflict resolution to handle the conflict. How will you begin the discussion?

A Word About Relatives and Friends

Sometimes others don't understand your child-rearing methods and may interfere with them. You can recognize their feelings and state your reasons for your actions. ("I understand you're uncomfortable with the way I'm raising Josh, but I find this works for me.") You may have to confront others and give them choices. ("I don't agree with treating Josh that way. It's discouraging. If you choose to continue, we'll stop visiting for a while until you and I can come to agreement.") This may be hard for you to do, but you have to decide what's best for your child.

---

*Don Dinkmeyer et al., *The Effective Parent* (Circle Pines, Minn.: American Guidance Service, 1987), pp. 113-14.

**Rudolf Dreikurs and Loren Grey, *A Parent's Guide to Child Discipline* (New York: Hawthorn, 1970), pp. 42-43.

CHAPTER 6

Effective Discipline

Realistic expectations, mutual respect, encouragement, communication skills—these form a framework for building cooperation and responsibility in young children. Within this framework, parents can find effective methods of discipline. Effective discipline helps children learn how to cooperate with others—and how to manage their own behavior. This chapter will discuss specific ways to discipline: setting limits for children and communicating expectations to them.

Reward and Punishment: Effective Discipline?

For many people, the word *discipline* means the same as *punishment*. Most of us were raised in families in which punishment—and its counterpart, reward—was the typical method used to discipline children. But this method doesn't offer children the chance to make choices so they can learn responsibility. And though reward and punishment may seem effective when children are young, it's a method that can have undesirable long-term consequences. Let's look at some of these effects.

Rewards

Rewards teach children that they have a right to expect payment for their cooperation. By relying on rewards, parents train children to behave in a certain way in order to *get* something—not to cooperate. Rewards must change in value as the child grows older. What motivates a two-year-old may not motivate a five-year-old.

Punishment

While rewards teach children to get, punishment teaches children to *resent*. Punishment guarantees a relationship based on fear. It is an attack on a child's self-esteem and usually invites rebellion.

Punishment may involve
- threats—which parents usually don't carry out
- yelling—which often teaches children not to pay attention unless parents scream!

When we reward or punish children, we teach them to look to an adult to be responsible for their behavior. Yet it is possible to raise cooperative children without rewarding and punishing them.

- overreaction—which may make problems worse by magnifying their importance
- put-downs—which include insults, name-calling, accusations, and unfavorable comparisons to other children
- withdrawal of privileges that have no clear relationship to the misbehavior—which creates resentment
- spanking

Spanking children shows them that it's all right to use hitting to solve problems. The message is, "If you're bigger, it's okay to get your way by hitting someone smaller." And giving children physical pain only teaches them to be afraid of parents. While spanking may stop misbehavior for a while, in time it loses its effect as a way to control behavior. Spanking may relieve a parent's anger, but most parents feel guilty afterward. Some children learn to use that guilt to get all sorts of privileges after a spanking.

When we reward or punish children, we teach them to look to an adult to be responsible for their behavior. Yet it is possible to raise cooperative children without rewarding and punishing them. Let's begin by defining *discipline*.

What Is Discipline?

If discipline is not rewarding or punishing children, what is it? Effective discipline is *teaching a learning process*. The goal of discipline is self-discipline: to guide children to be responsible and cooperative. Using this definition as a standard, parents can find many effective methods of discipline.

Methods of Effective Discipline

The keys to effective discipline are to establish mutual respect and to expect cooperation. Children respond to respect and positive expectations. The following methods can be used to discipline children effectively:

- **D**istracting the child
- **I**gnoring misbehavior when appropriate
- **S**tructuring the environment
- **C**ontrolling the situation, not the child
- **I**nvolving the child through choices and consequences
- **P**lanning time for loving
- **L**etting go
- **I**ncreasing your consistency
- **N**oticing positive behavior
- **E**xcluding the child with a time-out

The goal of discipline is self-discipline.

In selecting an appropriate method, it's important to consider a child's developmental level. Distraction, for example, is a useful strategy with babies, but time-out would be meaningless at this age. Structuring the environment for safety and positive experiences will mean something different for a crawling infant, a walking toddler, or a curious preschooler.

And, while a particular technique may be appropriate for most children of a certain age, you'll want to consider in each situation the developmental age and level of understanding *for your individual child.* You may discover that your toddler doesn't respond to time-out. You may learn that your preschooler is able to take on more or less responsibility depending on her mood. You will certainly find that, with your child, some methods are more effective than others.

Distracting the Child

Thirteen-month-old Sheryl scoots rapidly toward the lamp plug in the socket in the corner of the room. "Sheryl!" her mother calls firmly. Sheryl pauses and looks at her mother. Then her mother swiftly swoops Sheryl up in her arms in a friendly way and takes her to a toy in the opposite corner of the room.

Sheryl's mother uses an important skill of effective discipline—*distracting.* First she calls Sheryl's name to get her attention. Then she steers Sheryl to another part of the room and focuses the child's attention on something that is acceptable.

This is all done in a friendly, nonthreatening manner. If Sheryl heads for the lamp cord again, her mother can move swiftly, without words, and steer her toward another acceptable object. Acting without words avoids creating a struggle for attention or power.

If Sheryl is truly determined to get to the lamp plug and distraction isn't working, her mother could:

- take distraction one step further by moving to a different room to play, where the plug isn't a problem. A gate could be used to close off the room with the attractive plug.
- place her daughter in a playpen for a short while, for her immediate safety. This might be a necessary choice if Mother were busy with something for a while and just couldn't keep her eye on Sheryl every second.

Distraction works well with younger babies, too. It deals with their eager curiosity and short attention span in a respectful way. If you're holding your four-month-old and he suddenly pulls on your ear, give him something else to play with!

Ignoring Misbehavior When Appropriate

Three-year-old Colin wants a glass of juice. He has been told in the past that he will not be given what he wants if he does not ask for it respectfully. But Colin is feeling tired and crabby, and he whines for juice. His dad goes on fixing supper, and pays no attention to the request. Colin whines again, then remembers why he isn't getting what he wants. He says "please" and uses a pleasant voice when he asks a third time. His dad turns from his work and says, "I'd be happy to get you juice. I like the way you asked me."

Colin's father has used another skill of effective discipline—*ignoring misbehavior*. This skill can be used to handle minor disturbances that are not destructive or dangerous, such as showing off, sulking, whining, mild crying, temper tantrums, power plays, attempts to interrupt or beg for treats, and insults.

Of course, in some situations it would be inappropriate to ignore misbehavior. For example, your child is playing in a group and starts using bad language. Rather than ignore this behavior, you might decide to remove the child so the use of bad language doesn't spread to the other children.

Ignoring misbehavior involves more than not talking. If you still communicate your feelings by your facial expression or body language, your child will know you're not really ignoring her. If your child is old enough to be left alone, perhaps you could go to your bedroom or the bathroom for a few minutes. If you can't leave the room, concentrate on what you are doing rather than attend to your child. The misbehavior may get worse before it stops—most children don't give up easily. But your persistence will usually pay off.

Ignoring a behavior may be the most effective way to discourage it. But what we are ignoring is the behavior, not the child. When a child behaves appropriately, we give him attention—in this way we encourage the child without reinforcing a negative goal.

Structuring the Environment

Two-year-old Bonnie takes a piece of candy from the dish on Grandma's coffee table. Bonnie is told that one piece is all she may have. Grandma then puts the dish in the cupboard, and life goes on peacefully.

Bonnie's grandma is *structuring the environment* in her living room. She arranges objects and spaces to help Bonnie learn self-control and respect for property.

Structuring the environment sometimes goes by other names: childproofing or babyproofing. Babyproofing might also be useful in the case of Sheryl, whose mother wanted to distract her from going for the lamp cord. Sheryl's mother could unplug the lamp. Or, she might get a cover for the plug that fits over the outlet so the lamp can remain plugged in but be safer for Sheryl. A piece of furniture could also be moved in front of the plug and cord.

Young children need to explore in order to learn. It's up to us to structure the environment so that they can have more hands-on than hands-off experiences. By limiting the need to say no, we create a more positive atmosphere for children.

As soon as babies can move around on their own, it's time to childproof the environment. Well-known child expert Dr. Benjamin Spock suggests that rooms be arranged so your child can get to what's within his reach in three-fourths of a room. Then the forbidden zone is much easier for you to manage.[1] Have plenty of things your child can handle without causing harm to himself or distress to you!

Structuring the environment will mean something different for a crawling infant, a walking toddler, or a curious preschooler.

When structuring the environment, keep in mind that:

- Toddlers are in the process of learning the meaning of "my" and "mine." As your child learns to leave certain things alone, begin teaching the difference between "mine" and "yours."

  Two-and-a-half-year-old Chuck's father shows Chuck a special polished piece of driftwood. "This is mine," he says to his son. "Please ask before you touch it." Then he points to Chuck's well-worn stuffed lion. "Rex is yours," Dad explains. "May I hold him?" Chuck's father repeats this process from time to time, and Chuck is learning about ownership.

- As your child begins to respect your things, you can gradually include more of them in the environment. Children don't learn respect for the property of others if things are *always* kept out of reach. Of course, children will make mistakes in handling and using things that are not theirs. Bit by bit, though, they are learning self-control and respect for others' property.
- Setting predictable schedules and routines is another way of structuring the environment. Children feel more secure if they know what to expect. For example, breakfast follows dressing; lunch, snacks, and dinner are served at about the same time each day; and baths come before bedtime.

Controlling the Situation, Not the Child

Parents often fear that unless they control the child, the child will control them. Yet most children, like adults, want to feel in control. When we *control a situation,* we set guidelines and give the child freedom to choose within them. This in turn gives the child control—he has a choice, within the limits we've set. We're not controlling the child by telling him what to do, we're controlling the situation. When we let children control aspects of their lives appropriate for their developmental level, the chances rise of cooperation in areas where their choices are more limited.[2]

There are two ways to control a situation:

- By structuring the environment. The child is free to explore most spaces and objects in his environment. If he chooses to do something destructive or dangerous, parents can use distraction, remove the "off-limits" item, limit the space for free exploration, or remove the child, if necessary.
- By giving an older toddler or preschooler verbal choices within limits. "You may play quietly while I'm on the phone or leave the

room. You decide." You state the limits and your child's choices. If your child continues to be noisy, then she has chosen to leave the room.

Involving the Child Through Choices and Consequences

As children grow, they must learn to make decisions and take responsibility for their own behavior. Giving young children choices helps them begin to develop independence and cooperation. You can give simple choices that both respect children's desire for control and help you keep order:

- "Which of these toys would you like to take to Grandpa's?"
- "How many peas would you like—this many, or this many?"
- "Would you like to wear your red jammies to bed, or your blue ones?"

In a situation with choices, your child may say, "No, I want *this!*" Your reply can be, "That's not one of the choices." A similar approach can be taken when a child keeps changing his mind. For example, your child chooses an apple for a snack and takes a bite out of it. Then he decides he would rather have an orange. That's not one of his choices because the apple can't be reused.

Natural and Logical Consequences

When your toddler's or preschooler's behavior needs correction, you can use natural and logical consequences to give choices.[3] *Natural consequences* result from going against the laws of nature: The child who refuses to eat lunch gets hungry. *Logical consequences* are the result of going against the rules of social cooperation: If three-year-old Brad deliberately rides his tricycle into Kristen, Kristen may not want to play with him. Or an adult may take away Brad's trike-riding privileges for a while.

Natural consequences don't need any interference from adults. But many natural consequences are dangerous. For example, we wouldn't let a two-and-a-half-year-old run into the street to learn the danger of being hit by a car! Instead, we would set up a logical consequence: "The street's not for playing—you could get hurt by a car. You may play in the yard or inside—you decide. If you go near the street, I'll know you've decided to come in for a while." If the child decides to head toward the street, she has violated the limits. She has chosen to go into the house for a while. She may try the choices again a bit later. If she still goes near the street, she's chosen to play in the house again, this time for a little longer.

Logical consequences are the result of going against the rules of social cooperation.

Also, many situations don't have natural consequences, so logical consequences must be set up by an adult.

Logical consequences meet the needs of a particular situation. They have the following qualities:

1. They express the rules of social living. Consider this example:

You are talking with another adult, and your child enters the room to play. His play becomes noisy. You don't yell at him to be quiet or to get out of the room. You say, "I'm sorry, but we are trying to talk. Either play quietly, or go to another room to play."

2. They are related to the misbehavior. Again, consider an example:

Your three-year-old rides her trike beyond the boundaries she's been given. You don't tell her she has to go to bed early. Bedtime and trike riding are not related. Instead, you give her the choice of staying inside the boundaries, or not riding her trike for a while.

3. They separate the deed from the doer. Logical consequences don't imply that the child is bad because the child is misbehaving. Instead, they communicate, "While I don't like what you're doing, I still love you."

Your preschooler deliberately throws food on the floor. You don't yell at him or spank him. You simply assume he has finished eating and excuse him from the table.

4. They are concerned with what will happen *now*. Logical consequences are for dealing with the present—not with past misbehavior.

Your child wants to ask a friend over to play. The last time the friend came over, all they did was fight. You say, "You can invite Sam over as long as the two of you are willing to play nicely. If there's fighting, Sam will have to go home."

5. They are given in a friendly way. With logical consequences, parents can stress mutual respect by using a tone of voice and nonverbal behavior that show *firmness and friendliness* at the same time.

> *To her two-and-a-half-year-old, Mother doesn't say, "Get to bed quick, or else!" Rather, she says, "You need to go to bed now. Would you like to walk to your room or would it be fun to be carried?"*

6. They permit choice. With choice, the child has a stake in choosing responsible behavior, rather than being told how to behave.

> *To your two-year-old, you say, "You may play with the dog if you touch her gently. If you hit her, you will have to play with something else."*

Babies and Consequences

In most cases, logical consequences are not effective for babies. This is because babies are not yet ready to think logically. Of course, when there's a problem with a baby's behavior, there will be some kind of consequences. For example, if an infant pokes her father in the nose, he may hold her hand or place her on the floor so he won't be poked again. He can't assume, though, that a six-month-old, or even a one-year-old, understands the consequences of her behavior. However, the child does learn what to do or not to do. The child learns from the experience, though the learning may not be long-term.

Guidelines for Using Logical Consequences

Following a few guidelines can help make consequences effective.

Let the child's decision stand. When a child makes a decision, let the decision stand—for the moment. Later, give the child another chance to show that she is ready to cooperate.

> *Five-year-old Damita eats granola in the family room and leaves crumbs and an empty bag on the floor. The next time she has a snack, she's not allowed to take the food into the family room. But after that, she can try again.*

Some children *won't* decide. They may simply not know what they want. Or they may be trying to keep your attention or demonstrate power. When this happens, give the child the benefit of the doubt.

Three-year-old Melissa's stepmother offers Melissa a choice of snacks, and Melissa has trouble choosing one. "Think about it, Melissa," her stepmom tells her, "and then let me know what you decide." Ten minutes later, Melissa comes to her stepmother and says, "I still can't pick." "I tell you what," replies her stepmom. "I'll set the buzzer on the stove for ten minutes, and you decide by then." "But what if I still can't pick?" Melissa asks. With a friendly tone of voice, Melissa's stepmother tells her, "If you can't pick by then, I'll know you don't want a snack."

Children may be indecisive. Parents can help by letting the choice stand.

With repeated misbehavior, increase the time of the consequence. Each time the same misbehavior occurs, increase the amount of time for the consequence.

On her second chance, five-year-old Damita again makes a mess in the family room and doesn't clean it up. Now she is choosing not to eat in the family room for the next two snacktimes. (If the time until Damita can try again is not increased, she may be willing to accept not eating in the family room once, every time she makes a mess.)

Phrase the choice respectfully. Use a friendly and helpful tone. One way to phrase a consequence is to say, "You may _____, or you may _____. You decide."
- "You may settle down, or you may leave the room. You decide."
- "You can play nicely with Gerri or come for a walk with Daddy. You decide."

Another way is to say, "You may _____ if you _____."
- "You may play with the baby if you don't pinch him."
- "You can ride on my shoulders if you sit still."

A statement of your intentions or assumptions is also a logical consequence. It gives the child a choice in how to respond. "I'll help you if you'll ask me nicely." "If you're not dressed when the timer goes off, I'll assume you want to go to child care in your pajamas."

Respect the child's choice. Children will often choose the consequence to see if you mean what you say. This is the way they learn the limits. You can respect the child's choice by simply stating, "I see you've decided," or, "Your behavior tells me you've decided." Tell the child when he can have another chance to show that he's ready to cooperate: "You may try again   (state when) ."

Say as little as possible. Too much talk can ruin a consequence. When children misbehave, they expect parents to talk. Talking too much reinforces children's misbehavior goals. Say only what needs to be said, and then simply act.

By the same token, avoid nagging or threatening. The goal of letting your child choose is to *allow her to learn from her own experience.*

Make it clear when there's no choice. Giving a choice when there really *is* no choice sets the stage for problems. The same is true for open-ended choices. If, when it's time for a child to come in from playing, you ask, "Do you want to come in now?" you'll probably get a *no.* Instead, simply state, "It's time to come in now." If the child balks, give him a choice of how he wants to come in: "Do you want to come in on your own, or shall I help you?" Watch his behavior and act on his decision.

Keep hostility out of your consequences. If parents communicate hostility in any way, they'll turn consequences into punishment. Keep calm. Be both kind and firm. Show respect for yourself and your child.

Work on your feelings. Rehearsal is a good way to prepare to use a consequence. Practice saying the consequence in front of a mirror and with a tape recorder. Note your nonverbal behavior and your tone of voice. As you practice and become effective at giving consequences for misbehaviors that happen often, you'll find yourself more prepared for the unexpected.

Planning Time for Loving

All children need and want attention. Some parents pay attention to every positive and negative thing a child does. Others focus mostly on problems. But these two extremes teach children that they have a right to our attention whenever they want it. To counteract this, we can make an effort to spend *quality time* with our children. Spending quality time each day with each of your children—playing, cuddling, enjoying each other—is important to your child's emotional development, and to your relationship. It can also help prevent behavior problems.

Plan how to spend time with your children. Give each child your full attention when it's your time together.

Since two-year-old Anna was an infant, her mother has rocked her daughter and sung to her at night before bed. This has become a real sharing time, with Anna now singing along at first and requesting favorite songs. This ritual gives Mother and Anna fifteen or twenty minutes of close time each day that builds their relationship and helps Anna settle down for the night.

————

Four-year-old Bart and his dad are both early risers. Often in the morning they walk the dog together before Dad leaves for work. The morning walks give Dad and Bart regular time together and a pleasant start to their day.

Letting Go

As our children grow and learn to cooperate with us, we can show our confidence, and help build theirs, by learning to *let go*. When we show faith and confidence that our children can handle challenges appropriate to their ages and maturity, we build children's belief in themselves.

It can be hard to let our children stand on their own if we give or expect too much of certain qualities:

Protection. Children need protection, yet an overprotected child will lack self-confidence. She will feel unable to handle challenges.

A father can watch a crawling baby explore in the grass without being right beside her every second. A mother can let her two-and-a-half-year-old greet a friendly dog on a leash during a walk in the park. A five-year-old needs to learn to ride a bike, even if he'll take some tumbles in the process.

Obedience. We don't help our children or ourselves by trying to produce robots who obey our every wish. Children raised that way may become resentful and rebellious.

Permissiveness. Letting go doesn't mean parents should let children do as they please. When we are too permissive, we teach a child that he has a right to get whatever he wants, regardless of others' rights. Ask yourself, "Will permitting this behavior help my child learn to

> *When we show faith and confidence that our children can handle challenges appropriate to their ages and maturity, we build children's belief in themselves.*

cooperate with others?" If the answer is no, then you'll want to set limits on the behavior.

The final goal of parenting is to help our children become independent human beings who can act responsibly. Letting go at appropriate times and in appropriate ways is one way we help children do this. Like other aspects of parenting, letting go is a process that begins when our children are very young and continues as their responsibility increases over many years. As they demonstrate respectful behavior, we do more and more letting go.

Increasing Your Consistency

Children need discipline that is consistent. When parents treat the same behavior in the same way, no matter where or when, children will know what to expect if they misbehave. Work to *increase your consistency,* but also accept your limitations. No human being is *always* consistent.

Dealing with Misbehavior in Public

When you take a young child to any public place, it's important to have already established your way of handling misbehavior. We suggest that the discipline you use at home also be used at the store, in restaurants, and in the homes of friends and relatives. If you have one method of discipline at home and another outside the home, your child may learn to manipulate you when the two of you are away from home. But if you use the same discipline wherever you go, your child will always know his limits of behavior.

> *On a shopping trip, your preschooler wants a number of toys he has seen on television. You have already set rules about buying toys. Your child refuses to follow your rules and causes a fuss. You place him alongside you and go on with your shopping. But your child continues to misbehave. You stop shopping and head home. You respectfully tell your child that he will not go shopping with you again until he is ready to follow your buying rules.*

Taking young children to restaurants can be a problem. Begin with family restaurants that serve food children like to eat. Let your child bring along a small toy that will hold her interest. Behavior rules that apply at home also apply in restaurants. If the child misbehaves, her meal is over and it's time for a doggy bag. Sometimes, unfortunately, so is that of the entire group! To avoid this, one parent or another member of the group could take the child outside or to the car.

Whatever the problem, handling it as you would at home gives the steady consistency your child needs to learn to deal more calmly with change and stimulation.

Running errands and eating out are activities that can be very stimulating and stressful, especially for babies and toddlers. One of the best ways to deal with problem behavior of very young children in public is to avoid it. Make sure your child is rested and that it's not too close to mealtime before setting out on a shopping trip. If you plan to eat out, choose a restaurant that caters to families with small children.

Leaving your infant or toddler home while you run routine errands may not be an option, but you can make these trips more interesting to children by involving them in the task and making a game out of it.

> Children like to lick the stamps or drop the letters into the slot at the post office. They can enjoy identifying fruits and vegetables at the supermarket.

Dealing with Friends and Extended Family
It is hard to practice consistent discipline if you believe you need the approval of friends and relatives. Your child is not the measure of your self-worth. Suppose your child throws a temper tantrum at a gathering of your friends. You can remain firm in your method of discipline. Or you can give in and hope your friends don't notice your misbehaving child. If you give in, your child learns that he can get his way if he embarrasses you in front of others.

Like running errands and eating out, social gatherings and visiting other homes can be stressful. A baby may become more fussy than usual. A toddler may lose some self-control. Understanding this can help parents remain consistent in their approach. Whatever the problem, handling it as you would at home gives the steady consistency your child needs to learn to deal more calmly with change and stimulation.

Relatives and friends may criticize your discipline methods. They may interfere with your efforts by giving your child treats or privileges that you would not. Situations like these are challenging. You can be most effective by communicating your wishes to others in a friendly but firm manner. You may be surprised at how your own confidence inspires others to respect those wishes! If, on the other hand, the problem continues, for the sake of your child's training you may decide not to visit certain people for a while. This is an extreme response, however. The more respectful your approach, the more likely you'll be to win others' cooperation.

Dealing with Other Children

Preschoolers enjoy and need the sociability of other children. When playmates visit, though, discipline problems with your own child can surface. It is important that the same discipline applies when your child has company as when she is home alone. Although children's behavior often changes when other children come to play, it doesn't help if we accept misbehavior simply because another child is visiting.

Similarly, children who are guests in your home need to know the limits and expectations you have for their behavior. They may test an adult who is inconsistent in using discipline. Once children understand your rules of behavior—and realize that you mean what you say—they will be more willing to cooperate. If the rules are not followed, you may want to end the visit and send the guest home.

When Rules Are Different

Sometimes different rules in different places mean you can't be consistent.[4] This is frequently true with household rules. What you let your five-year-old do at home may be inappropriate when visiting others. Other people may have their own rules, and we need to respect those rules. You can explain: "At home, it's okay for you to play in my bedroom, but at Molly's, you only play where Molly's mother wants you to."

Noticing Positive Behavior

It's easy to spend a lot of time focusing on a child's negative behavior. But then the child begins to learn that negative behavior is a way to get attention, to belong. Limits are necessary, yet we can balance them with positive interactions with the child.[5] By *noticing positive behavior*, we can give our children more "yes" responses than "no" responses.

By noticing positive behavior, we can give our children more "yes" responses than "no" responses.

Besides the benefits such an attitude will have for children's self-image and confidence, it can also help prevent misbehavior. We can notice when children are cooperating with others: "Robbie, it looks like you and Ramón are enjoying playing together." It's especially helpful to comment on positive behavior soon after you've had to correct misbehavior. That helps a child learn you've rejected his behavior, but not him.

Excluding the Child with a Time-Out

Excluding with a time-out is a way to help a toddler or preschooler regain control of herself. It is actually giving a child time to calm down.

Use a time-out as a *last resort,* when other discipline methods haven't worked. A time-out is appropriate only for very disruptive behaviors, such as

- temper tantrums that can't be ignored and that are supposed to punish you or make you give in
- constant interference in your activities that can't be ignored (such as interrupting when you have guests)
- violent acts by a toddler or a preschooler (such as hitting or biting)

We also view a time-out as a choice. A child can choose to settle down or take some time out. A time-out is a form of logical consequences.

A time-out has two purposes:

- to teach the child he has to learn to control his behavior if he wants to be around others
- to give you a chance to keep control of your own behavior and emotions

The most effective time-out is for *you* to leave the scene. Make sure your child is in completely safe surroundings; then go to the bathroom or your bedroom. Don't come out until the child has calmed down. When you can't leave and you have to remove the child, follow these guidelines:

1. Select a location for the time-out. It needs to be away from people. The child's bedroom is a possibility. You may hesitate to use it for fear she'll view the bedroom as a prison. But if the time-out is initiated matter-of-factly, though, it won't be seen as a punishment. It's simply a means to give the child and you some quiet space. If you feel the child will be destructive, you can plan ahead and remove or put out of reach things you don't want destroyed. If the child destroys her own toys, that's a consequence she'll have to live with.

Some parents fear their child will kick the door or wall. But bruised objects can be repaired much more easily than bruised self-esteem! One caution: don't lock the door. If the child comes out of the room before the time limit, firmly but kindly return her to the room.

2. Explain the rules. Children need to know the rules of the time-out. When possible, it's best to give this information *before* a problem arises. Explain that when the child's behavior shows he's not ready to be with others, then he's chosen to take some time out. Tell him you'll set a timer. When he hears the buzzer, he can leave the time-out if he's ready to settle down.

3. Plan an appropriate length of time. Two or three minutes is plenty the first time. If the behavior continues after the child comes out of the room, add a minute for each new time-out. Usually make five minutes the maximum—that's a long time to a young child, even to a five-year-old. Eventually the child may be able to decide on her own when she's ready to come out, and you won't need the timer. You can tell her, "You may come out when you are ready to play nicely." In this way, she'll be developing internal control.

4. Allow the child to play. It's okay if you find the child playing in his room when the time is up. In fact, this shows he has regained some control. Remember, it's a time-out, not a punishment. Also, he doesn't have to come out of the room if he doesn't want to.

5. When a time-out is over, it's *over*. Don't discuss it. That would only call attention to the behavior you want to stop.

Provide Time for Training

One way to avoid troublesome behavior is to take the time to teach children skills they need to help them cooperate. Working with children in this way provides the positive attention they need. It helps them build skills, which in turn builds their self-confidence and opens doors to new experiences and responsibilities. Many areas that become behavior issues don't need to if parents have given the thought and time beforehand to guiding children in mastering skills of successful living.

Teaching and learning a specific skill or procedure needs to take place at a relaxed time. For example, trying to train your child to put on a shirt correctly during morning rush hour at your home will be a bad experience for both of you! When teaching any skill, make sure your child is interested and that it's a pleasant time for both of you. If either you or your child gets tired or bored, stop. Try it again some other time.

Training is often more effective with young children when you make it fun.

> *You tell your child you want to play a game and help him learn to dress himself. First, you have him put his clothes on backward, and laugh together about how that looks. You say, "That's how we would dress if we walked backward!"*

> *Next, you help him put on one piece of clothing correctly. Let him see how that looks.*

> *Then you have him choose the way to put on another piece of clothing. You encourage him when he does it correctly. If he puts it on wrong, you respectfully show him the correct way again.*

Getting this kind of enjoyable help in learning to dress can help your child cooperate in dressing himself during your morning routine. Of course, there's a chance he may decide to wear his shirt backward! If this happens, you might simply comment, "I see you've decided it's fun to dress backward!" Or you could tell your child, "It's fun to be silly—but we need to dress right today." A light, friendly tone should help you win his cooperation.

Discipline Is Teaching

Effective discipline calls on all our parenting knowledge and skills. As with any interactions with our children, patience and understanding will help see us through. If we keep foremost in our minds the meaning of discipline—to guide our children to develop self-discipline— we'll be able to keep a realistic perspective. Our helpful, respectful methods will offer our children many positive models for dealing with problems.

Notes

1. Benjamin Spock and Michael B. Rothenberg, *Dr. Spock's Baby and Child Care,* 40th anniversary ed. (New York: Dutton, 1985), p. 296.

2. Stanley Greenspan and Nancy Thorndike Greenspan, *First Feelings* (New York: Viking Penguin, 1985), p. 161.

3. Rudolf Dreikurs originated the concepts of natural and logical consequences. Rudolf Dreikurs and Vickie Soltz, *Children: The Challenge* (New York: Hawthorn Books, 1964), pp. 76-85.

4. Greenspan and Greenspan, p. 195.

5. Greenspan and Greenspan, p. 141.

Activity for the Week

Apply some of the effective discipline methods that are appropriate to the behavior, age, and maturity level of your child. Observe the results.

Chart 6

Logical Consequences for Misbehaviors

Babies

Many problem behaviors of babies can be dealt with more easily when parents understand the child's developmental needs and abilities. Infants need to explore in order to learn. Structure the environment so they can have more hands-on than hands-off experiences. Once your baby is mobile, careful childproofing is a must.

Toddlers and Preschoolers

Toddlers and preschoolers also need an environment that allows for hands-on experiences and is still childproofed. Keep in mind that all young children need to be given clear guidelines and limits.

Misbehavior Example	Consequence Category	Logical Consequence
Doesn't come to meal when called.	Denial or delay of activity	Matter-of-factly bring toddler to table. If toddler throws tantrum, remove to safe place. Don't feed again until regular snacktime. With preschooler, set timer. If not at table when timer goes off, not served.
Doesn't pick up toys.		Next activity delayed until toys picked up. (The younger the child, the smaller this task needs to be. A floor full of toys is too much for any toddler or preschooler to tackle alone. Parents can help or suggest one step at a time.)
Demands attention.	Loss of involvement	Adult ignores or leaves room.
Disrupts play group activity.		Child leaves area.
Handles an object inappropriately.	Denial of use of object	Show appropriate use. If misbehaves again, deny use of object for a while.
Loses or destroys own toys.		Guide toddler or preschooler in importance of putting toys away. Make sure toys are age-appropriate. Once these things are understood, do not replace lost or destroyed toys.
Causes disturbance on shopping trip.	Denial of access to places	Parent and child leave store, or child not taken on next shopping trip.
Makes mess eating snacks in family room.		Don't give toddler food to eat in family room—guaranteed mess. Don't allow preschooler to snack in family room if makes mess.
Doesn't feed pet.	Denial of cooperation	Toddlers are too young to remember on a steady basis, but can feed pet when told. Preschooler may need reminding from time to time. If no cooperation, child doesn't eat until pet is fed.
Demands help.		Help not given until child asks respectfully. If toddler is out of control with tantrum, help child calm down; then discuss.

Points to Remember

1. Effective discipline helps children learn self-control and cooperation.

2. Reward and punishment are not effective methods of discipline. They teach children to expect an adult to be responsible for their behavior.

3. In selecting an appropriate method, it's important to consider a child's developmental level.

4. Effective methods of discipline are
   - **D**istracting the child
   - **I**gnoring misbehavior when appropriate
   - **S**tructuring the environment
   - **C**ontrolling the situation, not the child
   - **I**nvolving the child through choices and consequences
   - **P**lanning time for loving
   - **L**etting go
   - **I**ncreasing your consistency
   - **N**oticing positive behavior
   - **E**xcluding the child with a time-out

5. Use natural and logical consequences to give choices to a child. Natural consequences result from going against the laws of nature. Logical consequences are the result of going against the rules of social cooperation.

6. Logical consequences
   - express the rules of social living
   - are related to the misbehavior
   - separate the deed from the doer
   - are concerned with what will happen now, not with past behavior
   - are given in a friendly way
   - permit choice

7. Guidelines for using logical consequences:
   - When a child makes a decision, let the decision stand—for the moment. Later, give the child another opportunity to cooperate.
   - Increase the amount of time for the consequences each time the same misbehavior happens.
   - When you give a child a choice, phrase the choice respectfully.
   - Respect the child's choice.
   - Say as little as possible, and avoid nagging or threatening.
   - Make it clear when there is no choice.
   - Keep hostility out of consequences.

8. Spending some quality time each day with your child is good for your relationship and can help prevent behavior problems.

9. Too much protection, permissiveness, or demands for obedience will prevent children from becoming independent.

10. A time-out is a form of logical consequences. Use it as a last resort, when other methods haven't worked.

11. Choose a relaxed time to teach skills, and make the training fun.

The Rights of Parents and Children*

Parents of young children may see themselves as all-sacrificing for the children. This attitude is stressful for the parents and unhealthy for the children. Children who grow up feeling they have to be the center of the universe have problems in relationships.

As a parent, you have the right
- to live your own life apart from your children
- to time for yourself and your adult relationships
- to friendships
- to privacy
- to respect for your property

A child has the right
- to be raised in a loving, safe atmosphere
- to have her wishes considered
- to be respected as a unique individual
- to a life apart from being the child in a family
- to privacy
- to respect for her property

The rights of both parents and children can be summed up in one phrase: the right to mutual respect.

What will you do this week to maintain your rights?
How will you show respect for your child's rights?

---

*Adapted from Robert T. Bayard and Jean Bayard, *How to Deal with Your Acting-Up Teenager: Practical Self-Help for Desperate Parents* (New York: M. Evans and Co., 1981), p. 95.

CHAPTER 7

Nurturing Emotional and Social Development

Throughout *Parenting Young Children* we've talked about the relationship between developmental level and behavior. Young children are developing physically, intellectually, emotionally, and socially. Healthy diet balanced with rest and appropriate physical activity can nurture children's physical growth. Intellectual growth is best served by encouraging learning that fits a young child's age, interest, and ability—not by pressuring or by a structured, academic approach.

What about emotional and social growth? We know that children also need our guidance to develop in these areas. We've examined ways to encourage positive growth through encouragement, open communication, building cooperation, effective discipline, and an environment of mutual respect. This chapter will look more closely at a few specific aspects of young children's emotional and social growth—particularly during the toddler and preschool years. It will discuss how we, as parents, can best support our children's development in these areas.

Understanding Young Children's Emotional Development

All of us have emotions. Emotions are involved in every experience we have. If we think for a minute about the challenges we adults face in handling our own emotions, we can appreciate what young children, with their limited experience, have to face in coping with theirs. Dealing with young children's emotions can be a challenge for parents. The most important effort we can make is to learn to empathize with—to be aware of and sensitive to—our children's emotions.

How fast children mature emotionally varies, both within an individual child and between children. Children's physical development is a continuous process, always progressing. But their emotional development can regress, as well as progress. A child may handle an emotion such as fear with some control one day. Then the next day, she may use no control over the same fear.

> *Three-year-old Ellen feels happy and confident as she comes home from the park with her dad. When a neighbor's large*

dog rushes up to greet them, Ellen responds calmly: "Doggie won't hurt us." The next day, Ellen takes the same walk home after having a bad afternoon. She feels cranky and unsure of herself. This time, she is scared when the dog comes toward her, and she clings to her dad. He says, "It's all right, Ellen. You feel afraid, but Rufus is only saying hello."

Children's emotional development is greatly influenced by a supportive environment and by our understanding and encouragement. We can take some specific steps to help our children develop healthy ways to express emotions:

- Use reflective listening to help children express feelings: "You seem unhappy." "You look confused."
- Fix any break in relationships with our children. For example, when you've been angry, you might say: "I'm sorry I was so angry. Let's talk about it."
- Respect each child's uniqueness: "You like to sing while you play with your blocks."
- Be aware of children's feelings and indicate clearly that we recognize and understand them: "I hear the thunder, too. It sounds scary."
- Interact and play with children. Play provides an opportunity to talk about feelings children may deliberately avoid. Puppets, dolls, and stuffed animals can all be used for role-playing.

> *Play provides an opportunity to talk about feelings that children may deliberately avoid. Puppets, dolls, and stuffed animals can all be used for role-playing.*

Four-year-old Judy's mother had been very sad since the death of Judy's grandmother. Judy had begun to misbehave frequently. One afternoon, Judy's father asked her to get her dolls so they could play together. "I wonder if your dolly has a grandma," he said to Judy. "Dolly's grandma died," Judy replied. As they played, Judy's father discovered that "Dolly" was alarmed to see her mother cry so much, and afraid that her mother had forgotten about her. Through play, Father was able to learn more about what his daughter was feeling and also to begin to help her understand and express those feelings.

- Help children see that it's possible to have confusing or contradictory feelings about a person—to love and be angry with someone at the same time: "Sometimes you like to play with Abel, but not when he fusses."
- Balance our understanding with appropriate limits: "I see you're angry because Glenda broke Dolly's arm. But people aren't for hitting. Come play over here till you're not so angry."

• Be aware of the importance of security objects. One way infants and small children cope with their emotions is by depending on objects. They may use their thumb or a special blanket for self-comfort. Thumb sucking can sometimes help a young child manage a situation. A child's caring for a doll, a teddy bear, or a blanket may increase his future capacity to love other people and other things.[1]

Emotions and Misbehavior

Between birth and age six, children don't outgrow the need to have their emotions understood. And they don't learn to cope with emotions most of the time. As they move through babyhood and into the toddler and preschool years, however, it becomes more likely that at times they will begin to use emotions to seek attention or power. Parents need to be sensitive to this and to kindly and firmly set limits.

> *Four-year-old Craig wants some cookies. His father says, "No, it's too close to dinnertime." Craig begins whining, "I'm hungry." Next, he starts yelling, "I want cookies! Give me some!" He continues his protest until his father loses his temper and sends Craig to his room.*

Craig's goal is power—he wants to have his own way. He uses emotions to try to reach that goal. The way Father has responded has stimulated more of the misbehavior he wanted to stop. If we understand *why* a child puts on displays of emotion, we will be less likely to be trapped by them—and less likely to respond with our own displays of emotion.

In the case of Craig, understanding that his son wants power can help Father decide to bow out of the power struggle. He can ignore Craig's whining and yelling or, if it becomes necessary to remove the boy from the room, can do so calmly and matter-of-factly: "I see you've decided not to stay in the kitchen, Craig. You may come back when you're ready to cooperate."

Emotional Challenges

There are countless challenges parents and children face when dealing with emotions. While we can't examine them all here, we can consider a few encountered by all parents of young children.

Crying

An infant's cry is her first verbal means of communication. Babies cry to communicate their physical and emotional needs. When they cry, they may be telling us that they're hurting or hungry or tired; that they're sad, angry, frightened, or lonely; or maybe that they've simply had too much excitement.

> *Sometimes, three-month-old Wendy wakes up crying during the night because she's hungry. Her mother nurses her, and Wendy falls asleep. Other times, Wendy wakes up crying, but*

her parents can find no physical reason for it. She isn't wet or hungry. Wendy just seems to need comforting to get back to sleep, and her parents gently rub her back for a while.

Toddlers and preschoolers communicate by crying, too. Because young children have difficulty putting their feelings into words, they often express some feelings by crying. Parents will want to comfort their crying children. But we can also be aware that tears and howls can become powerful tools! Children learn that emotional displays can be used to get attention or to engage a parent in a power struggle. Parents need to understand that children's crying can be an emotional trap. Because of crying, parents may give in to a child's demands, feel guilty, or lose their own emotional control.

> *Three-and-a-half-year-old Kordie likes to have her step-mother build blocks with her on the floor. Lately, when it's time to put the blocks away for bed, Kordie cries and hollers, "No—I want to play more!" Her stepmother feels irritated, and also a little guilty—especially because she works all day and doesn't have a lot of extra time to spend with Kordie. Playing longer stops the crying, but only until Kordie's stepmom again says it's time to quit.*

Kordie has found an effective way to keep her stepmother's attention. Unfortunately, letting Kordie win attention in this way is not helping her learn to deal with her feelings. This is a case where Kordie's stepmother would be wise to acknowledge her stepdaughter's feelings ("You're mad that we have to quit now, but it's bedtime") and matter-of-factly help her pick up the blocks and get ready for bed. Kordie's stepmother can also look for other ways to give positive attention when Kordie isn't demanding it—perhaps by enlisting Kordie's help to set the table for supper, or by noticing when Kordie "reads" to her little brother.

Certainly crying isn't always misbehavior. A careful look at the situation, and at their own feelings and responses, will help parents avoid letting children use crying to achieve negative goals.

Sadness

Like crying, sadness can at times be used by older toddlers and preschoolers to gain attention. When the lower lip comes out and the head goes down, parents are usually able to recognize whether a child

Because young children have difficulty putting their feelings into words, they often express some feelings by crying.

is seeking some special treatment. As with all attention-seeking children, parents can find ways to give attention when the child is not demanding it.

More often, though, sadness in a child is a cry for help. Such a cry cannot be ignored. Sadness may be a direct response to a loss—the loss of a friend, the death of a pet, or some other major disappointment. Help your child talk about such an experience while you listen to his feelings. Reflect and clarify what you hear from your child.[2]

Sadness may be a method a child has learned in order to manage her other feelings. Feelings of loneliness, inadequacy, anger, or depression may all appear on the surface to be sadness. It is important to determine the meaning and the purpose of a child's sadness. When dealing with a child who is sad, listen to her feelings. Take her seriously and treat her respectfully.

When a child seems sad for a prolonged period of time, parents will want to seek the advice of a pediatrician or professional counselor.

Jealousy

From about the age of eighteen months to three-and-a-half years, jealousy seems to be a particularly strong emotion for many children. During that time, a child may have to share parents' attention with a new baby. Also during that span, a child may start spending time at a child care center and have to share toys and attention with other children.

We can't totally get rid of jealousy in children, and it's not necessary to do so. Jealousy helps children face challenges in life, which in turn helps them mature. We can assist in making the jealousy less intense by helping children understand jealous feelings: "You're feeling angry because Daddy has to feed the baby now." "You're very sad when Rory goes to school and you don't."

It's not a good idea to leave a jealous toddler alone with a new baby.

When a new baby joins the family, young children often become jealous. The following guidelines may be useful when dealing with a child's jealousy of a new sibling:
- Make sure the child knows a new brother or sister will be arriving.
- Don't give excessive attention to the baby and ignore the older child. Your older child still needs your attention and private time with you. Let her know she's still a unique person to you.

- Get the older child involved in helping with the baby. Let her do tasks suited to her age level—bringing diapers or bottles, or helping feed the baby.
- A jealous child may become aggressive and may poke or hit the baby, disturb the baby's sleep, or hug the baby too tightly. It's not a good idea to leave a jealous toddler alone with a new baby.
- A jealous child may revert to babyish behavior to get your attention. He may increase his thumb sucking, talk in a babyish way, be cranky and demanding, or cling to you. Additional hugs will likely be more helpful than reprimands in easing this behavior.
- Have realistic expectations of your toddler or preschooler. Your having had a baby doesn't mean he is no longer a young child.

Fears and Anxieties

Children often express fear to indicate they need help. When children express such fear, parents can help best by being sensitive and supportive. Pediatrician T. Berry Brazelton has some suggestions for handling children's fears:[3]

1. Accept fears as part of the normal developmental process. If you react strongly to your child's fears, they will tend to increase. Then your child may become even more fearful. Instead, be matter-of-fact: "I know the noisy vacuum is scary. But it won't hurt you, and it helps me get the rug clean."

2. Understand why your child is fearful. Your child's fears need to be understood. They may allow him to control a situation, or to withdraw or not take part. Like other emotions, fear can sometimes be used by a preschooler to get attention or power, and it can be the start of aggression. Reassure your child that there are positive ways to be assertive, such as learning to express his feelings directly.

> *Driving to the first day of preschool, a mother says to her son, "I can tell you're nervous to be starting a new school. But kicking the back of the seat won't help. Why don't you tell me what you're thinking about while you kick?" "I'm thinking about my sandbox and trucks," he says. "I want to stay home and play with them." "There's a nice sandbox at the school," the mother replies. "And you can play in it with other kids. Won't that be fun?" "I don't know," he mumbles in reply. "I don't wanna go." "It's strange to start somewhere new," the mother says to her son. "I'll bet some of the other kids feel funny about it too. But I think you'll all have fun."*

3. Maintain the limits you've set and keep ordinarily acceptable boundaries. When your child is experiencing fears, don't reduce your limits and boundaries. Your child will learn to develop courage—the alternative to fear—by accepting these limits. There are many constructive ways to help the child overcome or lessen a fear; this too helps the child gain courage.

> *Four-year-old Warren has grown terrified of the dark. He refuses to go to bed, and has begun staying up later and later. Upset, his parents have stretched the limits further and now allow Warren to sleep with them each night.*

By letting Warren's fear take over, his parents are not helping their son cope with the fear. He may be sleeping securely in his parents' bed, but he isn't building courage or confidence in himself—and his parents have company every night! Instead, there are many constructive ways these parents might go about helping Warren overcome or lessen his fear. They might simply let him keep a light on in his room when he goes to sleep. Or, they could explore the room together before bed, making sure there are no "monsters" in the closet or under the bed. They could suggest he sleep with a special toy animal to keep him company. Over time, they can also discuss with Warren why he is afraid and whether his fears are realistic. It takes time to help children sort reality from fantasy.

4. Help your child become aware of outlets for feelings. Share how you, family members, and friends handle strong feelings. Introduce your child to sports, games, and other experiences for releasing aggression and expressing normal emotions. A child who has excessive aggressive feelings needs to learn additional ways to express them.

Some Common Fears
Children may feel fear or anxiety in a variety of situations. Some of the most common include the fear of animals, nightmares, and separation anxiety.

Fear of animals. A child can overcome some fear of animals by being around them. Let your child learn to play carefully with pets, and take her to the zoo to see different animals. Go slowly, and don't force her to get too close if she isn't ready. For example, a child may find it easier to get comfortable with a small dog than with a large one. You might also read books about animals with your child, to help her learn more about them.*

Nightmares. Frequent nightmares may be a sign that a child is upset about her relationships—with family, a new baby, or playmates. They may also show an unconscious goal of getting attention or power. A night-light or a talk about the dream may be helpful. If nightmares persist, you may want to seek professional advice about handling them.

Separation anxiety. To become a mature person, a child needs to learn to deal with separations. When you must leave your child, tell him you are leaving, explain when you'll be back, and then leave. Over time, he can learn to respect your need for separateness, just as you respect his.

> *Ten-month-old David cries loudly whenever his mother leaves him. He is learning about separation, and it is a frightening feeling. When David's mother is about to leave, she picks him up and gives him a big hug. She says, "David, you look sad and afraid because I'm leaving you for a while. It's okay to feel that way. You will be taken care of, and I'll be back soon." David doesn't understand all his mother's words, but he feels the empathy and respect for his feelings in her tone of voice and her body language.*

When a separation is longer—such as a parent starting a job—prepare the child for the change. One way to "practice" is to leave the child with the caregiver a few times before starting the job. With older toddlers and preschoolers, express clearly and positively what you will be doing: "I'm going to start a new job. While I work, you'll stay with Billy and Dee-Dee at Mrs. Herzog's." Encourage your child to let you know her feelings about the coming separation. Accept her feelings, but indicate that you are going to follow your plans.

A separation that often stimulates considerable fear for a child is starting preschool. This fear is normal. Your kind, but firm, confidence

---

*Reading books with children can be an effective way to help them build understanding and gain information. Libraries and bookstores offer a large variety of books appropriate for children from infancy on. For suggestions and descriptions of books you might read with your older toddler or preschooler, see *The Bookfinder, Volumes 1, 2, 3,* and *4,* by Sharon Spredemann Dreyer (Circle Pines, Minn.: American Guidance Service, 1977, 1981, 1985, 1989).

Watching their children mature, parents often develop their own fears and anxieties.

will help your child accept this separation. You can also visit the preschool before enrollment day and let your child meet the other children and the teachers. Encourage your child to ask you questions about the preschool.

Chapter 3 offers additional guidelines for choosing preschool and child care.

Parent Fears

Watching their children mature, parents often develop their own fears and anxieties. They may feel anxious as their children become independent, gain the ability to think logically, and show interest in the world.[4] But a child can't remain a baby. Parents want to encourage growth, not stifle it.

As parents, it is important that we deal with *our* fears and insecurities about our children's independence. We can begin by recognizing our mixed feelings about control—is it possible we may want to keep our children dependent?

For many years to come we will balance encouraging independence and setting limits. It's necessary to do both. As we encourage children to grow emotionally, we see that maturity and independence are possible. This can help us grow more secure.

Temper Tantrums

One of the most upsetting emotional behaviors is a temper tantrum— an explosion of rage from a child. Temper tantrums can leave a parent feeling angry, out of control, and embarrassed. They're even harder on a child.

There are two types of tantrums, and parents can respond to each in a different way.

1. Temper tantrums can communicate a child's frustration. A young child may be unable to express his feelings in words, or unable to do a task he wants to do. His sense of failure and rage explodes into a tantrum. It's best to let the child cry out this kind of tantrum. Often, trying to help him makes things worse. The child is battling with his own inabilities, and he must fight it out himself. When the tantrum is over, hold the child and comfort him: "It's hard to want to do something so much and you can't. But someday you'll be able to do it."[5]

2. Temper tantrums can be weapons used against parents. A child may throw a tantrum to gain power. She may be trying to force a parent to give in, or she may want to get even when she's denied something. It's best to ignore this kind of tantrum. If possible, leave the room. Attempting to comfort or talk to the child may simply reinforce her actions. If ignoring the behavior isn't possible, use a time-out. Later, when she's calmed down, talk about the feelings she expressed. "You were feeling very angry."

You may also try offering alternatives.

> *Brenda, a two-year-old, starts using tantrums to protest going to bed at the time set by her parents. In this case, if her parents leave the room and ignore Brenda's behavior, Brenda would get what she wants—avoiding going to bed. Instead, her parents offer her two alternatives: "Brenda, it's time for bed. You may choose to walk to your bed or be carried there." Then Brenda walks or is carried directly to bed. The tantrum may continue, but Brenda's parents will have responded in a way that doesn't reinforce Brenda's goal of power.*

The most effective way to deal with tantrums is to prevent them from happening. While this can't be done all of the time, there are many things parents can do to set the stage for fewer tantrums. Children often behave aggressively when they are tired and overstimulated. If you recognize that tantrums usually occur when your child is tired, hungry, overexcited, or frustrated in some way, then you can avoid this by steering her from situations that exceed her capabilities and by being aware of fatigue and hunger. At times you may also be able to distract your child from potentially tense situations and get her to relieve her tension in more acceptable ways—by running, jumping, or moving to music.

Stress

Stress is present in the lives of all young children. You can help control stress in your children's home environment by doing the following:
- Help children set realistic aims.
- Reduce competitiveness.
- Encourage children's efforts and any signs of progress.
- Create an atmosphere in which each child feels unconditionally accepted.
- Help children become contributing family members; for example, by doing chores.

- Help children learn simple relaxation skills, such as taking a deep breath.
- Listen to children's feelings.

One way children express tension is through physical symptoms. Brazelton believes each child has some organ that responds to stress by creating symptoms. These symptoms become outlets for pressures in the child's life.[6] Headaches or stomachaches may be symptoms of pressure in one child; colds or lingering coughs in another. Parents can deal with these symptoms by making sure the child feels understood and accepted, and by easing the stress. If any of these symptoms persist, the child should be seen by a doctor, who can determine other possible causes or suggest additional ways to relieve the stress.

Not all physical symptoms are caused by stress. Aches and pains that are sharp, get worse and more frequent, and include other symptoms such as vomiting or vision problems need to be treated by a physician immediately.

Understanding Young Children's Social Development

At the same time children are developing emotionally, they are developing socially. As children mature, they move toward independence. They begin to test their ideas of self and others in play and relationships. This move to independence appears to be built in to the maturation process.[7]

Maturing socially involves learning to deal with limits.

A child's steps toward independence are often challenged by dangers and new experiences. When parents use natural and logical consequences to set limits, the child learns from his behavior and feels secure enough to take more steps toward independence. Maturing socially involves learning to deal with limits.

Along with protection and dependence, children want separateness and independence. Interactions with other children let them test themselves socially. As they get older, children become more interested in interacting with others and learning the rules of the game.

Preschoolers and Sociability

Sociability comes with the preschool years. Between the ages of three and five, children interact with their peers more than ever before. They begin to learn what is socially acceptable and unacceptable.

Besides setting limits, parents need to focus on children's positive behavior. For example, a parent might say, "We need to be nice to people we play with," rather than, "Don't fight anymore!"

There are differences in the sociability skills of three-, four-, and five-year-olds.

Three-year-olds
- are learning to take turns. You may need to have children take turns and measure their turns with a timer.
- need to learn the importance of sharing. When children play together and there is one toy, they need to share it. You can say, "Willis, when you're through playing with the truck, please give it to Lyn. She would like to play with it." As your three-year-old learns to share, let him also have a few special toys that don't need to be shared with anyone. These can be put away when other children come to play.
- may still enjoy playing alone. Don't force a child to play with other children. Let her play alongside them.

Four-year-olds
- seem to have a great desire to play with other children. Your child may want to be at a friend's house or have the friend over all the time.
- have active imaginations. They often create imaginary friends, who may be human beings or animals. Such "friends" may also serve as a conscience for a child. Go along with the idea of your child's imaginary companion and play in pretend fashion.
- are determined and increasingly self-reliant. They tend to be domineering, and they appear to be self-sufficient. But don't be fooled into thinking your four-year-old is more mature than she really is.

Five-year-olds
- are beginning to become more settled, more serious, more poised.
- are developing positive feelings about their families.
- are growing in their ability to cooperate.

Encouraging Social Interest

One of the most important tasks of parents is teaching *social interest* to children. Social interest means caring about others and being willing to cooperate. It is based on mutual respect. Too many children learn

Criticism can stifle a cooperative spirit.

to expect others to serve them, instead of learning to be of service themselves. In your plan for helping your child become a responsible person, include specific attention to stimulating social interest.

Here are some suggestions that may be helpful for teaching social interest:

- Encourage your child's help at an early age. Let him do chores that match his abilities. Comment aloud about the importance of helping: "It's nice when someone helps with the dishes." "It feels good to help Grandpa, doesn't it? It's fun to see how happy he is!"
- As much as possible, let your child take care of his own mistakes—by picking up things he's dropped or cleaning up what he's spilled. If you automatically step in and do these things for your child, he won't as readily learn the value of cooperation.
- Don't expect perfection. Accept your child's efforts to do a task. This allows your child to feel free to take part, rather than hold back.
- Recognize efforts and progress. Encouragement is a wonderful way to build your child's interest in the world around him! An encouraged child will continue to reach out for new experiences, both independently and with other people.
- Don't change a child's first result—don't remake the bed just because your child left some wrinkles and lumps in it. Criticism can stifle a cooperative spirit.
- Have your child participate in family, religious, and community activities. Playing, working, and learning together—in a family meeting, a potluck supper, painting a neighbor's house—teaches active social interest.

Special Concerns About Social Development

As with emotional issues, social development involves many factors. While we can't touch on all areas, we've noted here five specific concerns of interest to most parents: honesty, dealing with aggression, toilet training, bedtime, and mealtime.

Honesty

We all want our children to be honest. With the preschool years parents often begin to see and hear things from their children that seem *dis*honest. Yet exaggerating and making up stories is typical behavior for preschoolers.

When children exaggerate, they are often telling us what they wish were true: "Look at me! I'm the strongest woman in the world!" We can acknowledge the wish behind the words: "You wish you were the world's strongest woman, don't you?"

Children also lie for the same reasons adults do. They want to get a good result or avoid a bad one. But young children don't see anything wrong with getting what they want, or with telling a lie to achieve it.

If your child lies, try not to overreact. Tell her it's important to tell the truth and that you're happy when she does so. You may want her to know you disapprove of lying to put the blame on someone else or to avoid responsibility. For example, "When I hear a story that isn't true, I feel worried. We need to talk about what really happened." At other times, you may simply choose to ignore her lying.

Exaggerating and making up stories is typical behavior for preschoolers.

Dealing with Aggression

We've all heard of "bullies." "Bully" is a label people commonly attach to someone who tries to dominate others to get his own way. As parents, we will probably have to deal with the problem of aggression at some time. The aggressiveness may come from our own children, or from others.

When another child is aggressive. Parents need to decide how to handle aggressive behavior. Children need to learn what options they have in dealing with someone who bullies them:
- Your child may have to avoid playing with the aggressive child.
- You may have to send the child away.
- Your child may need to become more definite about what he will or will not accept. Then he will need to face the other child and refuse to be a victim.
- You can aid your child by first helping him develop his courage within the family.

When your child is aggressive. If your child threatens other children, you need to understand the purpose of her behavior. It may be for power or control. Help her reach her goals in a more acceptable way. If your child continues to bully, she is choosing not to play with other children. She needs to be restricted. Persistent bullying may indicate a need for counseling.

Toilet Training

Trying to toilet train a child too soon frustrates both the child and the parents. Usually, a child isn't physically developed enough to control his bowel and bladder until the age of two or later.[8] This means that toilet training may be accomplished sometime between the ages of two and three. Be alert to your child's individual rhythms. It's important not to pressure him through any of the stages of toilet training.

You can follow some basic steps when toilet training your child:

- Give a young child word labels for bowel movements and urination. Names help the child understand what you are talking about. When you remove a soiled diaper, you might say, "Nancy has a BM in her diaper." Then teach her what she is doing when she is having a bowel movement: "Nancy is making a BM in her diaper."
- If your child has seen other people perform bathroom functions and tried to imitate them, he may be ready for a potty seat. Make one available. Watch for a few days to see if he shows an interest in using it. At first, encourage him to sit on it in a once-a-day routine. Don't pressure the child by expecting "results." Then have him sit on it a few times a day. When possible, have the sitting coincide with his usual elimination time.

Once your child is toilet trained, new problems may arise.

- Once your child uses the potty seat successfully for a few weeks, training pants are the next step. If you rush your child into them, she may feel terrified or uncomfortable and have an accident. Be cheerful about mistakes and setbacks. "Accidents happen. You can put on clean pants and try again." Bladder control usually comes sooner then bowel control. Daytime control happens sooner than nighttime control.
- Sometimes offering a specific remedy helps with bed-wetting: "How about not drinking a glass of water just before bedtime?" Don't wake your child for a trip to the bathroom. Waking him both puts pressure on him and takes the responsibility for getting up from him.

When toilet training, be cheerful about mistakes and setbacks.

Most children will be toilet trained by their third birthday. It usually takes boys longer to achieve control than girls. Treat temporary setbacks as unfortunate happenings, not big mistakes. Help the child get clean and dry, and show sensitivity and interest: "You must really be uncomfortable."

Bedtime

Young children need adequate sleep and regular rest periods. A specific bedtime and a regular, pleasant ritual for going to sleep have a positive effect on behavior. They are essential for a child's healthy development.

Many babies go to sleep willingly and regularly, as they feel the need. Often even a fussy baby can be helped to sleep simply by stroking her back for a while or rocking her gently. As they move into toddlerhood and the preschool years, children often find it hard to accept the idea of going to sleep. They may resist bedtime by making demands for a drink, a hug, a trip to the bathroom, or one more story. They may want to discuss some imaginary problem or fear. They may have slept too long or too late during an afternoon nap.

Parents may shorten and simplify the bedtime ritual by using these steps:
- Talk to your child earlier in the day about bedtime. Tell him you know he is old enough to sleep alone and you won't be staying with him.
- Start naps early in the afternoon and don't let them last more than an hour-and-a-half.[9]
- Anticipate as many of your child's bedtime demands as possible. When you have provided for all possible needs and requests, tell

the child kindly and firmly that this is the final good-night. Then follow through by not being involved any longer.
- Announce in advance that a story or a song is the last one and that you will be leaving the room.
- Once you have put your child to bed, don't respond to any additional calls for attention before she goes to sleep.

If your child wakes up during the night, begins to cry, and won't stay in his own bed, the following procedure may be helpful:
- Make sure your child isn't seriously frightened or sick, doesn't need a diaper change, and isn't thirsty.
- Put him back in his own bed, and leave the room. Don't put him in your bed and don't lie down with him in his bed.
- Firmly, kindly, and patiently repeat this process as many times as necessary. You'll need to do it fewer and fewer times each night.

Mealtime

Unfortunately, mealtime can set the stage for a growing, independent child to take a stand and exert her power. Here are some guidelines to help avoid having mealtime become a struggle:
- Have regular mealtimes and snacktimes, and avoid giving snacks at any other times. Rather than cookies or sugary drinks, provide nutritious snacks such as cheese, fruit, or fruit juice at regularly scheduled times.
- Expect a young child to spend no more than fifteen or twenty minutes at the table. After that, the child may be excused and the food put away.
- Provide small amounts of food. When the child has eaten those, give him more. If he begins to play with the food, his meal has come to an end.
- Avoid emphasizing food as a factor in your relationship with your child. Offering food as a reward or insisting on a "clean plate" can set the stage for the supper table to become a battleground.
- Prepare a variety of foods for your family. Consider the child's preferences, but don't start a pattern of fixing only certain foods or making "special" meals for one family member or another. Trying to find out what a child will eat or what he wants to eat will give him attention and power instead of good nutrition.
- Have rules about when and in what amount sweets can be eaten.

Offering food as a reward or insisting on a "clean plate" can set the stage for the supper table to become a battleground.

The Courage to Meet Challenges

Much of *Parenting Young Children* is really about courage. The principles and methods presented all help develop courage in children. We want our children to be courageous—to be willing to meet challenges and solve them.

Courage isn't just for our children. Raising children is a challenge, and parents need courage to face that challenge successfully. You are courageous when you are firm, but fair, with your child, and when you stand up for your own beliefs but also understand your child's beliefs.

It can be tempting to give children pity, sympathy, and too much help. We don't like to see them struggling or hurting, and we enjoy doing things that please them. Yet the most loving gift we can give our children is the opportunity to grow and become responsible, cooperative, and self-reliant. By creating an atmosphere of respect, we sow the seeds of mutual respect. Through a knowledge of their individual needs and capabilities, we learn to set realistic expectations. By offering encouragement and positive communication, we build their confidence and understanding of self and others. And by balancing children's freedom with appropriate limits, we discipline and we foster self-discipline. With all these actions, we are building children's courage.

Our own patience, understanding, and self-acceptance can help us through the ups and downs of parenting. As we help our babies, toddlers, and preschoolers grow, we also set the foundation for a lifelong parent-child relationship built on love and mutual respect.

The most loving gift we can give children is the opportunity to grow and become responsible, cooperative, and self-reliant.

Notes

1. T. Berry Brazelton, *To Listen to a Child: Understanding the Normal Problems of Growing Up* (Reading, Mass.: Addison-Wesley, 1984).

2. Brazelton, pp. 45-63.

3. Brazelton, pp. 41-42.

4. Stanley Greenspan and Nancy Thorndike Greenspan, *First Feelings* (New York: Viking Penguin, 1985), p. 37.

5. T. Berry Brazelton, *What Every Baby Knows* (New York: Ballantine, 1987), p. 66.

6. Brazelton, *To Listen to a Child*, pp. 131-32.

7. T. Berry Brazelton, *Toddlers and Parents* (New York: Dell, Delta Books, 1974).

8. Brazelton, *To Listen to a Child*, p. 162.

9. Brazelton, *To Listen to a Child*, p. 121.

Chart 7

My Plan for Meeting My Parenting Challenges

Use this chart to plan parenting strategies and assess progress. Begin now to chart and work on at least one challenge.

Child's name:_____

Challenge 1:_____

What I've been doing about it: _____

_____

My beliefs that interfere with progress: _____

_____

My plan for meeting the challenge: _____

_____

_____

My progress:_____

_____

_____

Challenge 2:_____

What I've been doing about it: _____

_____

My beliefs that interfere with progress: _____

_____

My plan for meeting the challenge: _____

_____

_____

My progress:_____

_____

_____

Points to Remember

1. Your child's emotional development is influenced by a supportive environment and your understanding and encouragement. Be aware of, and sensitive to, your child's emotions; also set appropriate limits. Recognize that children may choose emotions to get attention, power, or revenge or to display inadequacy.

2. Young children unable to use words use crying to express their feelings and needs. They may also use crying to control parents.

3. Sadness in a child may be a response to a loss or a way to manage other feelings. Listen and show you understand. Help the child be aware of the feelings.

4. Jealousy can be particularly strong in children ages eighteen months to three-and-a-half years. It most often occurs when a new baby arrives in the family.

5. To help your child handle fears and anxieties:
   • Accept fears as part of normal development.
   • Understand why your child is fearful.
   • Don't change the limits and acceptable boundaries you've set.
   • Help your child learn appropriate outlets for feelings.

6. A temper tantrum may come from a child's frustration at her inability to use words or do a task. Let the child cry out this kind of tantrum; then comfort her. A temper tantrum may be a weapon against parents. Ignore this kind of tantrum or use a time-out.

7. All young children have stress in their lives. They may express tension through physical symptoms such as headaches or stomachaches.

8. Children between the ages of three and five begin to learn what behavior is socially acceptable and what is not. Set limits, but also focus on children's positive behavior.

9. Stimulate your children's social interest. Teach them to care about others, to be of service to others, and to be willing to cooperate.

10. Lying and exaggerating are normal for preschoolers. They lie to get a good result or avoid a bad one, or to say what they wish were true. Don't overreact to lying.

11. If your child is bullied, he needs to learn what options he has in dealing with the aggressive child. If your child is the aggressor, understand the purpose of his behavior and help him reach goals in a more acceptable way.

12. Don't try to toilet train a child too soon. Children usually aren't physically ready for it till age two or later.

13. A specific bedtime and a regular, pleasant bedtime ritual have a positive effect on children's behavior.

14. Don't let mealtime become a power struggle between you and your child.

15. Children need to develop courage—to be willing to meet challenges and solve them. Parents need courage to face the challenge of child rearing.

Just for You

Dealing with Your Emotions

Emotions are actually a form of thinking. We create our own emotions by thinking certain things to ourselves. First, we tell ourselves how we, other people, or life *must* or *should* be. Then, when we, other people, or life don't follow our orders, we become upset—often overly upset.

Twelve common beliefs can cause us problems:*

1. I *should* be perfect.
2. I *should* be the best.
3. I *should* win.
4. I *should* succeed.
5. I *should* always be in control.
6. I *should* please everyone.
7. I *should* be right.
8. I *should* make a good impression.
9. People *should* give me my own way.
10. People *should* recognize my contribution.
11. Life *should* be fair.
12. Life *should* be easy.

If you hold some of these beliefs, you may see negative events as catastrophes rather than simple annoyances. Instead of believing you, others, and life are worthwhile, you may then blame yourself, others, or life for negative situations. You will tend to think you can't handle a situation, even though a more useful belief would be that you *can* handle it, even if you don't like it.

The key to changing these negative patterns of thinking is to decide there's no reason why things *should* be as we want them. If we recognize and believe this, we're less likely to become overly upset. We may feel annoyed or disappointed, but we won't feel that each disappointment is a catastrophe.

If you find yourself strongly upset, check the twelve beliefs above. See if you can find a belief that's causing you distress. Then take these steps:
- *Decide* to look at the situation as unfortunate, not as catastrophic.
- *Decide* to accept imperfections, not to blame.
- *Decide* you can take what life dishes out.
- *Decide* there's no rational reason why any person or situation should follow your orders.

Accepting these decisions will change your feelings.

To learn more about thinking and emotions, read Albert Ellis and Robert A. Harper, *A New Guide to Rational Living* (Englewood Cliffs, N.J.: Prentice Hall, 1975) and Albert Ellis and Irving Becker, *A Guide to Personal Happiness* (North Hollywood, Calif.: Wilshire Book Co., 1982).

---

*Don Dinkmeyer, *Self-Encouragement and Self-Hypnosis: A Route to Self-Mastery,* and Gary D. McKay, *Self-Confidence: How to Get It and How to Keep It,* audiocassettes (Coral Springs, Fla.: CMTI Press, 1987, 1985—write to CMTI Press, Box 8268, Coral Springs, FL 33075-8268).

To Learn More About Parenting

The method of child rearing presented in this book is based on a program called Early Childhood STEP (Systematic Training for Effective Parenting of Children Under Six). Four STEP programs are available:

- Early Childhood STEP (based on this book, *Parenting Young Children*)—for parents of infants, toddlers, and preschoolers
- STEP—for parents of preschool through middle school children (also available in a Spanish-language edition, PECES—Padres Eficaces con Entrenamiento Sistemático)
- STEP/Teen—for parents of junior high and high school youth
- The Next STEP—for parents who wish to extend the skills taught in the other STEP programs

Parents who have taken part in STEP programs report favorable results:

- increased knowledge of parenting
- improved relationships in their families
- better communication with their children
- less conflict in their families

STEP programs are effective because they offer parents support and encouragement. Members of a STEP group meet other parents who face the same challenges and share the same concerns. They all learn and practice new parenting skills with mutual support and cooperation.

If you are interested in joining or leading an Early Childhood STEP, STEP, STEP/Teen, or Next STEP group, many organizations in your community may be able to give you information. Check to see if groups are being offered by local schools, community centers, health centers, churches and synagogues, adult education programs, counseling centers, civic groups, psychologists, social workers, or the military.

For additional details about any STEP groups in your area, or for information about how to start a group yourself, write to the publisher:

AGS®
American Guidance Service
Publishers' Building
Circle Pines, MN 55014-1796

In Canada, write to:

Psycan Corporation
P.O. Box 290, Station V
Toronto, Ontario M6R 3A5

In Australia, write to:

Australian Council for Educational Research Ltd.
P.O. Box 210
Hawthorn, Victoria 3122

Index